Phlegmatic-Choleric
Workbook

The Inspector Pattern

How To Develop Your Natural Tendencies and
Deal With Your Strengths and Weaknesses
Biblically

John T. Cocoris, Th.M., Psy.D.

© Temperament Dynamics, LLC
4848 Lemmon Ave.
STE 152
Dallas, TX 75219

www.fourtemperaments.com
info@fourtemperaments.com
512-553-8104

Library of Congress Card Number:
ISBN 978-1-94-84-74-37-5

Temperament Dynamics, LLC
Dallas, Texas 75219

Cover design and interior design and layout by
John T. Cocoris

Printed in the United States of America

Acknowledgements

I am indebted to my wife, Darrellene, who has shared my vision and my passion for the four temperaments. She has reviewed this manuscript and made suggestions that made it better. I am indebted to my brother, Mike, for his guidance and support. He is my mentor. I am also grateful for Phillip Moss with whom I have spent countless hours talking about the temperament concept of behavior. He has made suggestions that have contributed to the completion of the workbook series.

John 3:16

For God so loved the world that He gave His only begotten Son,
that whoever believes in Him should not perish
but have everlasting life.

Table of Contents

Table of Contents

PREFACE

I began my journey in 1977 to understand and develop the temperament model of behavior. Along the way I have been a pastor, a corporate consultant, and a professional therapist. I am grateful for the opportunity to have worked with corporations, churches, and those with whom I had the privilege to counsel and coach.

I have written a number of books and manuals on the subject of temperament. This work includes insights that I have observed while working with thousands of people in different settings that are not in my other writings.

Previous books include an explanation of all the temperament blends, one on the creative temperament, one for parents, another identifying the seven steps for learning to apply the temperament concept, another explaining why Christians seek counseling, and even one explaining why girls chase guys after a breakup.

A book on how to develop the natural strengths and deal with the natural weaknesses has been requested many times and is long overdue.

A workbook for each temperament blend is a culmination of my life's work that includes my theological training, my experience as a corporate consultant, and my experience as a professional therapist.

This workbook is written for Christians. It is my heart's desire that as you read and apply the information, and the Biblical applications, that you will grow in the grace and knowledge of Jesus Christ and become more like Him.

John T. Cocoris
McKinney, Texas

Temperament knowledge is to life
what oil is to a machine,
it makes it run smother.

John 13:34-35

A new commandment I give to you, that you love one another:
just as I have loved you, you also are to love one another.
By this all people will know that you are my disciples,
if you have love for one another.

Author's Note

I have written a series of books and manuals on the subject of temperament. Each work represents a different application of the temperament concept. In order to adequately understand each application it is necessary to include in each work a variation of the history of the temperament concept, foundational principles, and common questions. If this is the only book you read on the subject of the temperaments then you would need the information in Part I. The material found in Part I is also found in more detail in my book, Why We Do What We Do, New Insights Into The Temperament Model of Behavior, 2020. This work contains excerpts from other books that I have written.

This workbook is design for someone that has takened the Four Temperaments Assessment. You can take the assessment by going to www.fourtemperaments.com.

Matthew 18:21-22

Then Peter came up and said to Him, "Lord, how often will my brother sin against me, and I forgive him? As many as seven times?" Jesus said to him, "I do not say to you seven times, but seventy times seven.

PART I

The History & Development of The Four-Temperaments

*You are **not** a product of
your environment or
circumstances,*

*you are a product of
your **choices**.*

Chapter 1

Introduction

The concept of the four temperaments does not appear in the Bible. We can, however, see the behavior of the four temperaments in the men and women of the Bible.

Temperament

Each temperament has both strengths and weaknesses. By knowing your temperament blend you will be more aware of your natural strengths and natural weaknesses. There are steps provided that will help you use your natural strengths and overcome the impact of your natural weaknesses on yourself and others.

The Goal is Christ Likeness

The goal of this workbook is to help Christians, using the knowledge of their temperament blend, and Biblical concepts, to grow spiritually and to become more like Christ.

Three Separations

Most people do not understand why they behave the way they do. There is a disconnect within that is perplexing. Many have asked, "Why did I do that?" The answer is a combination of having a sin nature (as a result of Adam's sin) and possessing natural tendencies referred to as temperament. The consequences of Adam's sin is three separations which occurred immediately after he sinned:

1. Separation from God (Genesis 3:1-11).
2. Separation from the woman (Genesis 3:12, 20).
3. Separation from within himself (Romans 7:19-20).

    Jeremiah 17:9 *The heart is deceitful above all things, and desperately wicked; Who can know it?*

    Romans 7:19-20 *For the good that I will to do, I do not do; but the evil I will not to do, that I practice. 20 Now if I do what I will not to do, it is no longer I who do it, but sin that dwells in me.*

As a result we do not understand our internal motivations and drives. Knowing your temperament blend identifies that which is normal and natural which will enable you to first become *aware*, and then *control*, specific thoughts, feelings, and behaviors on your spiritual journey to become more like Jesus Christ.

Be Doers

This workbook will offer Biblical principles for you to put into practice. **James 1:22** says, *But be doers of the word, and not hearers only, deceiving yourselves.*

Johari's Window

The Johari Window, named after the first names of its inventors, Joseph Luft and Harry Ingham, is one of the most useful models explaining our awareness or lack thereof. A four paned "window," as illustrated below, divides personal awareness into four different categories, as represented by its four quadrants: open, blind, hidden, and unknown. The lines dividing the four panes are like window shades which can move as more self-awareness is achieved.

Admittedly, it is a difficult thing to really know yourself (much less someone else). Few people take the time to even try to figure out *why they do what they do*. Most seem content not to know even though they may wonder. Some live their life in the dark never really understanding themselves or being aware of their behavior and how it impacts others.

People have different levels of self-awareness. There is the *open self*, this part of a person is known to yourself and to others. There is the *concealed self*, this part is not known to you, but known to others. There is the *secret self*, this part is known to you, but unknown to others. Then there is the *invisible self*, this part is unknown to you and others. This reveals that there are naturally some things you do not know about yourself. Some things remain a secret, even to you.

Known to Self	Unknown to Self
OPEN	**BLIND**
Known to Others	Known to Others
Known to Self	Unknown to Self
HIDDEN	**UNKNOWN**
Unknown to Others	Unknown to Others

It is helpful, enlightening and encouraging, to discover the natural tendencies with which you were born. This information may open the *window* and allow you to see something about your *concealed* and *invisible* self.

The purpose of this workbook, in part, includes you becoming more *aware* of the expression of your natural temperament tendencies. Being more aware take *ownership* of your natural tendencies to consciously express the controlled strengths and develop a plan to overcome the negative impact of your weaknesses on yourself and others.

Chapter 2

History of The Four Temperaments: Significant Contributors

Throughout history there have been many attempts to explain *why people do what they do*. One of the first systems developed was astrology which looked *outside* of man to explain behavior.

The idea that a person's behavior is the result of being born with natural traits or tendencies (temperament) has been around for at least 2,400 years. However, there is evidence that it's been around much longer than that.

Those listed below are the pioneers that have made the most significant contributions to the development of the temperament model of behavior.

Hippocrates of Kos (C. 460-377 B.C.)

Hippocrates, the father of modern medicine, looked *inside* of man to explain the differences in people's behavior. He taught that behavior (temperament) was determined by the presence, in excess, of one of four *biles* or *humors*:

Yellow Bile | An excess of yellow bile (Chlor) resulted in a temperament (Choleric) believed to be warm/hot and dry and associated with the element of fire.

Red Bile | An excess of red bile (Sangis) resulted in a temperament (Sanguine) believed to be warm/hot and wet and associated with the element of air.

White Bile | An excess of white bile (Phlegm) resulted in a temperament (Phlegmatic) believed to be cool/cold and wet and associated with the element of earth.

Black Bile | An excess of black bile (Melan) resulted in a temperament (Melancholy) believed to be cool/cold and dry and associated with the element of water.

The word temperament comes from the Latin word *temperamentum* and means "right blending." Hippocrates postulated that an imbalance among the four biles/humors resulted in pain and disease and that good health was achieved through a balance of the four biles/humors. For many years this idea was held as the foundation of medicine.

Since the time of Hippocrates the temperament concept was used as the basic explanation for *why people do what they do*. The temperament concept lost popularity when modern psychology began in 1879.

Hippocrates and the early Greeks were accurate in their observations of behavior but were incorrect about the origin of these tendencies. These tendencies are not, of course, created by the presence of a fluid. Today, we would say that they originate from some genetic predisposition although we cannot be certain.

Galen of Pergamon (AD 129-200 or 216)
Galen was a Greek physician who lived 600 years after Hippocrates and was responsible for popularizing the temperaments during his time and relating them to illness. He is also credited with coining the terms Choleric (from Chlor), Sanguine (from Sangis), Phlegmatic (from Phlegm), and Melancholy (from Melan).

Nicholas Culpeper (1616-1654)
He was the first to dispute two fundamental concepts that had existed since the time of Hippocrates. First, he rejected the idea that the four "humors" were the cause of a person's temperament. Secondly, he was the first to say that a person is influenced by two temperaments, one primary and one secondary. Before Culpeper, it was believed that a person had only one temperament.

Immual Kant (1724-1804)
He described the four temperaments in his book, *Anthropology from a Pragmatic Point of View*, 1798. These excerpts are from his book and shows the consistency and enduring nature of human behavior:

The Choleric Temperament of The Hot-Blooded Man. We say of a choleric man that he is fiery, burns up quickly like straw-fire, and can be readily appeased if others give in to him; there is no hatred in his anger, and in fact he loves someone all the more for promptly giving in to him.

The Sanguine Temperament of The Volatile Man. A sanguine person is carefree and attaches great importance to each thing for the moment, and the next moment may not give it another thought. He is a good companion, high-spirited, and all men are his friends.

The Phlegmatic Temperament of The Cold-Blooded Man. Phlegma means apathy, dullness; phlegma as weakness is a tendency to inactivity, not to let oneself be moved even by strong incentives for getting busy. He is not easily angered, but reflects first whether he should get angry.

The Melancholy Temperament of The Grave Man. A man disposed to melancholy attaches great importance to everything that has to do with himself. He finds grounds for apprehension everywhere and directs his attention first to the difficulties. The melancholy temperament thinks deeply.

Kant taught that a society should be based on appreciating the temperament differences in people.

William Moulton Marston (1894-1949)

Dr. Marston was the first to contribute scientific evidence that people fit into one of four categories. He studied the emotions of normal people and through his research identified four distinctively different behavioral responses to specific environments and people. He then selected 35 words or phrases that represented the four different approaches.

Marston's research determined that when a person is faced with a *favorable* or *unfavorable* situation two things happen. First, there is a neurological event caused by the perception of the stimuli in the environment (favorable or unfavorable). Second, a message is sent to the motor self (that which causes movement) to either move toward the stimuli, to move away from the stimuli, or not move at all.

He published his book *Emotions of Normal People* in 1928 using the terms Dominance, Inducement, Submission, and Compliance. Here are the four categories and the summary of his research:

Dominance [Choleric] This person has active, positive movement in an unfavorable (antagonistic) environment to overcome the opposition to get their desired results.

Inducement [Sanguine] This person has active, positive movement in a favorable or friendly environment to enjoy socializing.

Submission [Phlegmatic] This person is passive in both a favorable and unfavorable environment.

Compliance [Melancholy] This person has two responses in an unfavorable (antagonistic) environment. The *first* response is to withdraw. After the situation has been analyzed and a plan developed, the *second* response is to be assertive to bring resolve. In a favorable environment they will move forward to enforce the rules and offer organization.

Here are a few little known facts about Dr. Marston: he was also responsible for the invention of the *systolic blood-pressure test* which he attached to the current version of the *lie detector*. He also created the cartoon character, *Wonder Woman*.

Ole Hallesby (1879-1961)

Ole Hallesby, a Lutheran theology professor in Norway, contributed penetrating insight into the behavior of the four temperaments. He wrote *Temperament And The Christian Faith*, 1940; he used the terms Choleric, Sanguine, Phlegmatic, and Melancholy.

The book by Hallesby is limited in that he discusses behavior as it relates to the four *primary* temperaments and did not write about the dynamics of the combinations. However, his insights into the behavior of the temperaments are unsurpassed in the writings that I have reviewed. For the serious student of the four temperaments this book is a must read.

Hans J. Eysenck (1916-1997)

Dr. Eysenck in *Personality and Individual Differences, A Natural Science Approach,* 1985, (p. 3), sums up the concept of temperament this way:

> This was pioneered by Hippocrates and later canonized by Galen, a Roman physician who lived in the second century A.D. It is to these men and to the many others who worked in this field that we owe the doctrine of the four temperaments: phlegmatic, sanguine, choleric, and melancholic. The highly successful typology thus established all those years ago was based on careful observation and provided a paradigm for scientific investigation that has lasted over 2,000 years and may still have something to teach us.

Dr. Eysenck has written other books on the subject including, *The Biological Basis of Personality* (1967).

Tim LaHaye (1926-2016)

Tim LaHaye was the first to popularize the temperament concept within the Christian community. Dr. LaHaye published the first of several books in the 1960's using the terms Choleric, Sanguine, Phlegmatic, and Melancholy. He was the first to write in detail about the dynamics of the temperament blends.

John G. Geier (1934-2009)

John G. Geier built on the previous works of William M. Marston (1928), Walter Clarke (1940), and John Cleaver (1950). Walter Clarke developed the *Activity Vector Analysis* using the four dimensions of Aggressive, Sociable, Stable, and Avoidant.

Building on Clarke's work, John Cleaver created the first 24-question, forced-choice instrument. Building on the works of these men, John Geier developed the *Personal Profile* instrument in 1972 (later called the *Personal Profile System,* 1977) that identified an individual's behavioral style. John Geier coined the terms High D (Dominance), High I (Inducement), High S (Submission), and High C (Compliance). He created the acronym DiSC.

John Cocoris (1943-Today)

Dr. Cocoris built on the works of those who have been mentioned plus his own research. He developed the DISCII, DISC3, *discstrengths,* and *fourtemperaments* assessments. He pioneered the development of a system to verbally validate a person's temperament blend. His research and writings were based on personally interviewing thousands of people all across the USA. He has published numerous books and manuals on the subject of temperament and is the author of this work.

Others

Others have contributed to the concept of *temperament* including Plato (350 BC), Paracelsus (1530), Adickes (1905), Spranger (1914), Kretschmer (1930), Adler (1937), Fromm (1947), Eysenck (1951), and Keirsey (1970).

TEMPERAMENT MODEL DEVIATIONS

The researchers mentioned above have maintained the original concept that there are four categories of behavior. They have expanded our knowledge with their observations and insights. There have been others, however, who have deviated from the historical flow by adding concepts that have caused confusion rather than clarity. Included in these, in my opinion, are Carl Jung and Isabel Myers. Both have been criticized for their lack of clarity and apparent contradictions.

The original observations made over thousands of years have been proven to be consistent and accurate. Any system that deviates from it is incomplete, sometimes incorrect, and even misleading. Virtually all current approaches represent fragments of the four temperaments without a reference to the history from which it is based.

Carl Jung (1875-1961)

Carl Jung, a Swiss psychiatrist, published *Psychological Types* in 1921. He was searching for answers as to why people were different. The premise of his work was to determine how people take in information and make decisions.

Jung coined the terms *extrovert* and *introvert* (1921) suggesting that everyone falls into one of the two categories. The extrovert prefers the outer, objective world of things, people, and actions. Whereas the introvert prefers the inner, subjective world of thoughts, ideas, and emotions.

Jung identified four mental functions that he combined with *extroversion* and *introversion*: thinking (logical, objective); feeling (subjective experience); sensation (stimuli from the senses); and intuitive (creative, imaginative and integrative). Jung's system has eight basic personality types: extroverted thinker, extroverted feeler, extroverted sensor, extroverted intuitor, introverted thinker, introverted feeler, introverted sensor, and introverted intuitor.

There is some correlation between Jung's system and the original four temperaments by Hippocrates but at best it is not clear. However, Jung made a valuable contribution by giving us the concepts of *extrovert* and *introvert*.

Isable Myers (1897-1980), Katherine Briggs (1875-1968)

Isabel Briggs Myers and her mother-in-law, Katherine Cook-Briggs, wrote a paper in 1958 titled, "Myers-Briggs Type Indicator (MBTI)" in which they proposed that there are sixteen different personality types. Their work was based on Carl Jung's writings on psychological types. In their system, a person has two choices for orientation; introvert (I) or extrovert (E); two choices for method of information intake sensing (S) or intuition (N); two choices for method of judgment, thinking (T) or feeling (F); and two choices to use in the outer world of judgment (J) or perception (P). These combine to make up 16 personality types.

The Myers-Briggs Type Indicator is a popular and widely used instrument but it is not without controversy. David J. Pittenger, Ph.D., made the following comments in his evaluation of the MBTI:

> There are several reports of the test retest reliabilities of the four dimensions of the MBTI (Carskadon, 1977, 1979; Howes & Carskadon, 1979; Stricker & Ross, 1962). These

reports offer a consistent pattern that suggests that the reliability of the MBTI does not meet expectations derived from its theory" (Cautionary Comments Regarding the Myers-Briggs Type Indicator, published in 2005 in Consulting Psychology Journal: Practice and Research, Vol. 57, No. 3, 214).

The Myers Brigg Type Indicator does not allow for a person to be a combination of an *Extroverted* (E) and *Introverted* (I) combination. This is a major error of the MBTI assessment.

The temperament model of behavior demonstrates that a person can be an extrovert/introvert or introvert/extrovert combination; for example, the Sanguine-Melancholy is an extrovert/introvert combination and the Melancholy-Sanguine is an introvert/extrovert combination.

Summary. The ancient Greeks observed people and speculated on the reasons for their behavior. Their observations were supported in later centuries by a wide variety of people including medical doctors and philosophers.

In the early 1900's, the scientific method was applied by Marston with the same results. The concept that people fall into four categories has been observed for over two thousand years, verified by the scientific method, and everyone describes them basically the same. The four temperament model illustrates the consistency and enduring nature of human behavior.

Chapter 3

Frequently Asked Questions

1. WHAT IS TEMPERAMENT?

Temperament is Not The Same As Character

Temperament has nothing to do with a person's character or their level of maturity. It is what a person is naturally. Here is my definition:

> **Temperament is a cluster of inborn traits that causes you, in part, to do what you do.**

Temperament is Not a "Type"

A distinction needs to be made between a "trait" and a "type." "Types" are considered to be categories into which a person may either *fit* or *not fit*. For example, a person could be seen as either an *extrovert* or *introvert*.

Temperament Represents a Cluster of "Traits"

Temperament is a cluster of inborn traits that causes you, in part, to do what you do, naturally. Temperament, therefore, represents the core foundational tendencies or drives that make up an individual.

The four temperaments are represented by four distinct groups of traits or tendencies. Each cluster of traits produces a distinct manner of behavior that is different from the other three groups. For example, the Choleric is result-oriented, the Sanguine is people-oriented, the Phlegmatic is service-oriented, and the Melancholy is quality-oriented.

Each trait can be placed on a continuum from low expression to high expression. For example, one may possess the trait of being social to a high degree, moderate degree, or almost not at all. A trait is like a rheostat switch that controls a light. When you turn the switch up the light gets *brighter,* when you turn the switch down the lights gets *dimmer*. The more of a given trait one possess, the more observable it will be in their behavior.

The temperament model embraces the trait approach which allows for a particular trait to be possessed and developed to varying degrees. Temperament represents natural traits or tendencies with which a person is born. How well these natural traits are developed depends on the individual's choices.

Arnold Buss and Robert Plomin (1975) give Gordon Allport's definition of temperament in *A Temperament Theory of Personality Development*:

Temperament refers to the characteristic phenomena of an individual's nature, including his susceptibility to emotional stimulation, his customary strength and speed of response, the quality of his prevailing mood, and all the peculiarities of fluctuation and intensity of mood, these being phenomena regarded as dependent on constitutional makeup, and therefore largely hereditary in origin.

John Geier (1983), in *The Library of Classical Patterns*, describes temperament this way:

During a lifetime we experience many emotions, but there is an emotional state which is most characteristic for each of us. We depart from that basic temperament when aroused by such feelings as love, hate, sadness, anger, rage, or exuberance. However, these emotions tend to be as transient as they are intense. Love slips through our fingers; hate is difficult to sustain for long periods; joy and sorrow eventually dissipate. Like strong winds, these emotions temporarily ruffle the surface of our usual emotional demeanor. When others describe us with such words as friendly, logical, aggressive, or careful, they are referring to the feeling state we usually project. That state reflects our self-concept and has evolved from genetic predispositions and the shaping forces of the environment. Others may approve or disapprove of our temperament. It may meld or conflict with the expectations of groups or organizations. The crucial aspect is recognizing the "given" of our emotions and choosing the environment in which we will be accepted and productive.

Temperament Behavior is What a Person is *Most* of The Time

Temperament behavior represents the way a person relates to others and responds to events. It is what you have observed and expect someone's behavior to be.

Have you ever referred to someone as shy or outgoing? Without realizing it you were referring to certain temperament traits. These traits are what you know and expect the person to be every time you are with them. Thus, temperament behavior is, for the most part, predictable. The exception being when one temporarily experiences strong emotions, such as anger or fear, or is trying to deceive another. Actually, acting is a form of acceptable deception. A person is knowingly acting like they are someone else. Unfortunately, some purposely act like someone they are not in order to deceive.

Society would not be able to exist if behavior were not predictable. Imagine what life would be like if everyone were different every time you met them. Imagine the chaos. Without consistency in people, without predictability, any society simply would not survive.

Temperament is a *Drive*

Temperament is a *drive* or *force* within that represents various traits or tendencies that produce an *urge* that creates an *appetite*. Temperament urges and even drives a person to act in a particular manner. Temperament, as an appetite or void, requires satisfaction. An obvious illustration is when you are hungry you have a need to eat; it's a void to be satisfied. When you eat, the void is filled and you are satisfied and no longer hungry. Temperament is that way. It pushes or urges you to behave according to the tendencies that represent your temperament combination.

For example, there are those who are naturally *people-oriented*. They enjoy being with, around, or just standing by others. They like to talk, have fun, and be active with others. There is a drive/force within these people that urges them to do this. Ask those with the Sanguine temperament and they will tell you "I just like being with people." Conversely, there are those who are private in nature and they prefer *not* to be with, around, or by others. There is an equal force within them that urges or drives them to avoid contact with others. Both are normal drives that urge a person to meet their natural yet different needs.

Temperament is a *Need*

Abraham Maslow says that a *need* is something that if not met will make you sick. Air, food, and water, are physical needs without which a person would become physically ill and die. Temperament represents needs but no one will die without those needs being met. A temperament *need* represents what is important and highly desirable in the core of an individual.

Temperament is a *need* that urges, drives and motivates a person to act according to their natural tendencies. If temperament *needs* are not met, the individual will not feel at peace or function efficiently. Meeting temperament *needs* is, therefore, critical to a person's sense of well-being and feeling of self-worth.

Let's again use the Sanguine temperament as an example. As a *people-person* the Sanguine enjoys social involvement. This includes talking to others or just being in the presence of one or more people. Social contact is a *need* of the Sanguine temperament and if not met the person will not feel okay about themselves. This is just one of the four temperaments. The others will have specific *needs* as does this one but all will be different from each other. The Choleric, for example, *needs* to see results quickly; the Phlegmatic *needs* to follow a routine; the Melancholy *needs* to have a detailed plan. These *needs* are both normal and natural. Everyone, therefore, should provide adequate satisfaction for their temperament *needs* in order to be at their best.

2. FROM WHERE DID WE GET OUR TEMPERAMENT?

There are two possibilities. Either people are born *without* natural tendencies or they are born *with* natural tendencies.

People Are Born *Without* Natural Tendencies

Some believe that people start life as a blank slate (tabula rasa) and that the environment determines their personality. Dr. James Dobson (1987) is not in favor of this position but reports it in *Parenting Isn't for Cowards*:

> Sigmund Freud, the father of Psychoanalysis, and J.B. Watson, the creator of behaviorism, believed that newborns come into the world as "blank slates" on which the environment would later write. For them a baby had no inborn characteristics of personality that

distinguished him from other infants. Everything he would become, both good and evil, would result from the experiences to be provided by the world around him. He could make no independent decisions because he had no real freedom of choice ... no ability to consider his circumstances and to act rationally on them. Watson even rejected the existence of a mind.

The view that tendencies are acquired was also stated by David Merrill and Roger Reid (1981) in *Personal Styles & Effective Performance*:

Why do people develop these behavioral preferences? ... people tend to do things that make them feel comfortable. Once a pattern of actions receives positive reinforcement, we have a tendency to repeat it.

People Are Born *With* Natural Tendencies

This position teaches that a person is born with natural tendencies and that they are developed according to the person's response to their environment. In the article "Born to be Shy?" Jules Asher (1987) wrote the following concerning Dr. Jerome Kagan's research:

We've all met shy toddlers — the ones who cling to their parents and only reluctantly venture into an unfamiliar room. Faced with strangers, they first freeze, falling silent and staring at them. They seem visibly tense until they've had a chance to size up the new scene. Parents of such children are likely to say they've always been on the timid side. 'It's just his way,' one might say.

Arnold Buss and Robert Plomin (1975) discuss this position in their book, *A Temperament Theory of Personality Development*:

To aid understanding, we shall start with a non temperament model of personality. This model assumes that each person starts as a blank slate (tabula rasa) that will be written on by experience. It assumes that man's nature is that he has no nature. It flatly rejects the possibility of inborn tendencies that determine individual differences in personality. Environment is all. If there are stable individual differences, they are learned during childhood, during adulthood, or both. We have no quarrel with this model if it is restricted to some aspects of personality. There is presently no basis for assuming that differences among persons in self-esteem, guilt, or authoritarianism are derived from inborn dispositions. These and many other aspects of personality would seem to be wholly acquired during the course of living. But we cannot accept this model for all aspects of personality. Some behavioral tendencies - we would argue, some of the most basic personality tendencies - originate in inherited dispositions.

Dr. James Dobson (1987) discusses temperaments in his book, *Parenting Isn't for Cowards*:

> It is my supposition that these temperaments are prepackaged before birth and do not have to be cultivated or encouraged. They will make themselves known soon enough. Behavioral scientists are now observing and documenting the subtle understandings that have been evident in Scriptures for thousands of years. One of the most ambitious of these efforts to study temperaments of babies has been in progress for more than three decades. It is known as the New York Longitudinal Study, 1969. The findings from this investigation, led by psychiatrists Stella Chess and Alexander Thomas, are now reported in their excellent book for parents entitled, *Know Your Child*. To my delight, Chess and Thomas found that babies not only differ significantly from one another at the moment of birth, but those differences tend to be rather persistent throughout childhood.

In their book *Personality Structure & Measurement*, Dr. Hans Eysenck and Sybil Eysenck (1969) state that traits are rooted in genetics:

> These early ideas developed by Greek writers, thinkers and physicians already contain, if only in embryo, the three main notions which characterize modern work in personality. In the first place, behavior or conduct is to be described in terms of traits which characterize given individuals in varying degrees. In the second place, these traits cohere or correlate and define certain more fundamental and more all-embracing types. In the third place, these types are essentially based on constitutional, genetic or inborn factors, which are to be discovered in the physiological, neurological and biochemical structure of the individual.

Dr. Tim LaHaye (1977), in *Understanding the Male Temperament*, says, "The combination of inherited traits he receives from his parents at the time of conception will determine his eventual temperament."

Finally, perhaps the best proof of all is to ask a mother who has raised at least two children. She will likely tell you that they were different from birth. My daughter has twin girls and knew before they were born that one was going to be active and the other one was going to be laid-back, and that is exactly how they are today.

3. WILL MY TEMPERAMENT BLEND EVER CHANGE?

No. The temperament blend you were born with remains throughout your life. Some are confused about this because they think that because they have experienced some growth that their temperament blend somehow has changed. When in fact all that has happened is they have learned self-control and have matured. There are three areas to consider:

Temporary Modification

There are times when your behavior does not represent your temperament blend but this will always be temporary. A situation may require that you behave in a way that is not natural for you to act, but when the need has passed you will once again behave in a way that represents your temperament blend.

Growth

On occasion, some report that their temperament has changed over the years (e.g., once "shy" and now "outgoing"). I have found this to always be a person with a combination of an extroverted and introverted temperament (e.g., Choleric-Phlegmatic, Sanguine-Melancholy, etc.). There is a way of behaving which you feel is right, good and normal. This represents your "temperament comfort zone" of behavior. When a person suggests that their temperament has changed, they usually mean they had been driven out of their "temperamental comfort zone" by forces in their environment and did not develop their natural tendencies. During their developing years their behavior was represented more by their secondary temperament than their primary one.

We are all influenced by many variables, such as the quality of early home life, education, travel, etc. Regardless of these early influences, as a person develops, they begin to feel more "comfortable" with the way they want to be and are willing to actually behave in that manner. It is not that their temperament has changed, it is simply that they are now expressing the behavior they have always wanted to, they are in their "temperamental comfort zone."

Permanent Modification

It is possible for anyone to control their natural tendencies so that their behavior is modified and does not reflect a particular weakness. For example, the Sanguine has a tendency to talk a lot. Until they learn to moderate the need to verbalize, it can be annoying to others. Once they become aware of this weakness, they can choose to not talk as much thus gaining control over this weakness.

4. ARE TEMPERAMENT AND PERSONALITY THE SAME?

No. They are many factors that make up the total personality of a person. Temperament is only one of the many parts. Stella Chess and Alexander Thomas comment in their book, *Know Your Child*:

> But this recognition of the importance of temperament should not lead to an attempt to equate temperament with personality. We consider personality to be a composite of the enduring psychological attributes that constitute the unique individuality of a person. Personality structure is formed from the many diverse elements that shape psychological development, all acting together: motivations, abilities, interest, temperament, goals and value systems, psychological defense mechanisms, and the impact of the family and the larger sociocultural environment. Temperament is one of the important factors that helps to shape personality, and its influence varies from person to person. Because temperamental

categories or patterns evidence themselves as responses to environmental events and attitudes, the final results of such interactions vary from one person to another. In some instances, one temperamental attribute or pattern may be important in personality development, in other cases a different temperamental attribute may be significant, in still other cases the important temperament pattern may be different again.

5. CAN ANYONE BE A LEADER OR MANAGER REGARDLESS OF THEIR TEMPERAMENT?

Yes. Each person will lead differently according to their temperament blend. The Choleric and Sanguine will lead by *inspiration* (they will *tell* you how to do it). The Phlegmatic and Melancholy will lead by *example* (they will *show* you how to do it). Each one will be effective in their own way. Consider the following Presidents of the United States: Choleric, Donald Trump; Sanguine, Ronald Reagan; Phlegmatic, Gerald Ford; Melancholy, George W. Bush.

6. ARE THE FOUR TEMPERAMENTS IN THE BIBLE?

The Bible does not specifically address people according to this concept nor does the word *temperament* appear in Scripture. The four temperaments are, however, represented in Biblical characters: the Apostle Paul, Choleric; the Apostle Peter, Sanguine; Abraham, Phlegmatic; the Apostle John ,Melancholy.

7. HOW DO THE DIFFERENT NAMES CORRELATE?

There have been many different terms used to refer to the four temperaments. Below is a correlation of some the more popular ones: My personal preference is to use the most archaic terms when referring to the four temperaments; Choleric, Sanguine, Phlegmatic and Melancholy. A descriptive term alone is too narrow, restrictive and limits one's understanding of that particular temperament. A descriptive term will only *suggests* what the person may do in certain situations, it does not represent the essence of the temperament.

For example, a common term used to refer to the Choleric is "Dominant." The Choleric can be dominant but they are not dominant all the time. The term limits our understanding of the Choleric temperament. A common term used to refer to the Sanguine is "Expressive." Indeed they can be expressive but they will not be this all the time. The term limits our understanding of the Sanguine temperament. A common term used to refer to the Phlegmatic is "Amiable." It is true that they can be "amiable" but it is also true that they can stubbornly resist being cooperative. The term limits our understanding of the Phlegmatic temperament. A common term used to refer to the Melancholy is "Compliance", suggesting that they will always be this way. It is true that they can be "compliant" but it is only true if they respect the authority. The term limits our understanding of the Melancholy temperament. A more general term, however, allows for a broad expansion of understanding of a particular temperament. The use of the terms Choleric, Sanguine, Phlegmatic and Melancholy does not bring a narrow bias to the temperaments and leaves open a broad understanding. The point is that a term should not limit understanding or "tag" a temperament with a narrow description.

Correlation of terms.

There have been many different terms used to refer to the four temperaments. Here is a correlation of some the more popular ones:

Choleric	Sanguine	Phlegmatic	Melancholy
High "D"	High "I"	High "S"	High "C"
Dominant	Influencing	Steadiness	Compliance
Directive	Interactive	Supportive	Corrective
Driver	Expressive	Amiable	Analytical
Director	Socializer	Relater	Thinker
Red	Yellow	Gray	Blue

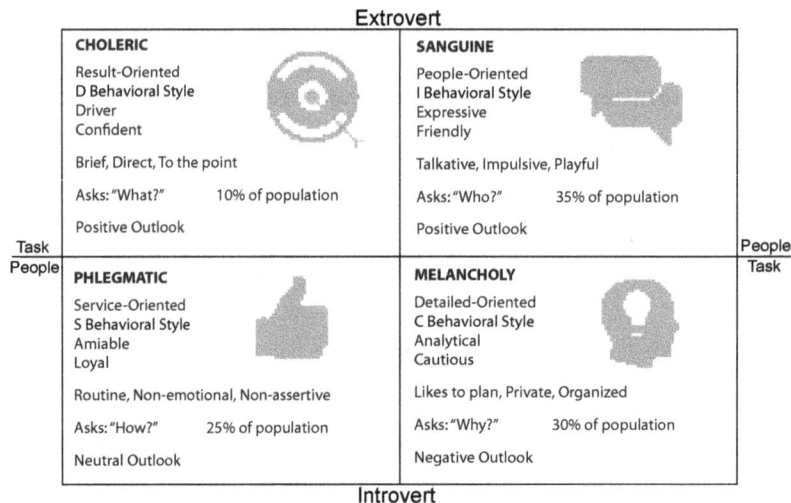

Extrovert

CHOLERIC	SANGUINE
Result-Oriented	People-Oriented
D Behavioral Style	I Behavioral Style
Driver	Expressive
Confident	Friendly
Brief, Direct, To the point	Talkative, Impulsive, Playful
Asks: "What?" 10% of population	Asks: "Who?" 35% of population
Positive Outlook	Positive Outlook

Task / People — People / Task

PHLEGMATIC	MELANCHOLY
Service-Oriented	Detailed-Oriented
S Behavioral Style	C Behavioral Style
Amiable	Analytical
Loyal	Cautious
Routine, Non-emotional, Non-assertive	Likes to plan, Private, Organized
Asks: "How?" 25% of population	Asks: "Why?" 30% of population
Neutral Outlook	Negative Outlook

Introvert

Summary. The ancient Greeks merely made observations about human behavior and speculated on its causes. Their observations were supported in later centuries by physicians and philosophers. In the early 1900's the scientific method was applied by Marston, with the same results. The concept has been observed for centuries and verified by science, that people fall into four categories, and everyone describes the four the same.

PART II

THE
Inspector

Phlegmatic-Choleric

The better you feel about yourself

the better the world looks!

Chapter 4

The Phlegmatic Temperament

The Phlegmatic temperament has three combinations: Phlegmatic-Choleric, Phlegmatic-Sanguine, and Phlegmatic-Melancholy. The traits of the *primary* temperament, Phlegmatic, will be altered or modified in some significant way because of the influence of the *secondary* temperament. The Phlegmatic is a frequently occurring temperament.

The Phlegmatic is naturally service-oriented. They are passive in both favorable and unfavorable environments. They influence their environment by cooperating with others to carry out the task. They tend to not be highly ambitious and they tend to lack a sense of urgency (both due to their passive nature).

The Phlegmatic is introverted, calm, unemotional, easygoing, indecisive, patient, and agreeable. They are both slow and indirect when responding to others. The Phlegmatic is slow to warm-up but will be accommodating in the process. They are by far the easiest people with whom to get along — as long as you do not try to alter their routine or ask them to change.

The Phlegmatic lives a quiet, routine life free of the normal anxieties of the other temperaments. They avoid getting too involved with people, and life in general, preferring a private, low-key life-style, centered around home and family. A mother who has the Phlegmatic temperament will often refer to her children as "My children" leaving a bewildered look on her husband's face.

The Phlegmatic will rarely exert themselves with others or push their way along in their career. They just let it happen. They make good team players. They communicate a warm, sincere interest in others, preferring to have just a few close friends. They are possessive of their friendships and material things. The Phlegmatic will be very loyal to their friends. They find it difficult to break long-standing relationships regardless of what the other person does or doesn't do. However, once a relationship is broken they seldom return.

The Phlegmatic strongly resists change. They need time to adjust when change does occur, especially sudden change. They avoid conflict (which is why they are so accommodating). They resist making quick decisions. The Phlegmatic is a practical, concrete, and traditional thinker. Their stoic expression often hides their true feelings. They can be grudge holders. The Phlegmatic can also be patient to the point of paralysis. They are persistent, and consistent, at whatever they undertake. Because of their passive nature they tend to easily procrastinate.

The philosopher Immanuel Kant in his book, *Anthropology from Pragmatic Point of View* (1798), says this about the Phlegmatic:

> Phlegma [Phlegmatic] means *apathy,* dullness; Phlegma as *weakness* is a tendency to inactivity, not to let oneself be moved even by strong incentives for getting busy. A man

who is insensitive to such stimuli is voluntarily useless: his inclinations tend only to satiety and sleep. Phlegma as *strength,* on the other hand, is the quality of not being moved easily or *rashly* but, if slowly, still *persistently.* The man with a good portion of phlegma in his constitution warms up slowly but retains his warmth longer. He is not easily angered, but reflects first whether he should get angry.

The theologian Ole Hallesby in his book, *Temperament & The Christian Faith*, says this about the Phlegmatic:

> The phlegmatic has the calm, well-balanced temperament. In the first place, impressions from his surroundings have a far more harmonious effect on the phlegmatic individual than they have on the other temperaments. There is no one side of his nature that is especially active.

The following represents behavior of the Phlegmatic in general. Individual differences will occur based on the influence of the second temperament and their level of maturity. Also, what a person is exposed to from an early age plays a vital role in these areas but remember an individual is still responsible for the choices they make. Regardless of one's natural tendencies, discipline applied in any area will control and overcome a weakness or extreme behavior. The goal is to become a well-balanced person being in control of thoughts, feelings, and behavior.

Relationships

The Phlegmatic builds a limited number of relationships slowly and will usually never let go regardless of what the individual says or does. Once they become your friend they will be loyal, dependable, and faithful. However, as mention earlier, they seldom repair a broken relationship. They do not have a wide social network preferring to have a few close friends and, of course, their family.

The Phlegmatic will take awhile to warm up and may never be the affectionate, warm, cozy, "sit by the fire" type. They respond well to a low-key, peaceful relationship.

Time Management

The Phlegmatic tends to be a poor manager of time. They lack a sense of urgency so they will often put off doing a task. They so want to accommodate everyone that it will paralyze them from getting something done in a timely manner. However, if they establish a routine of being on time early in life, they will follow it consistently. The Phlegmatic tends to not be in a hurry so they experience less stress and live longer.

Money Management

The Phlegmatic views money as *security* because of their tendency to excessively worry. They are reluctant to spend their money because they do not have a need for the latest anything or to replace what they bought years before. When they buy furniture for their home it could sit there for twenty years (or more) and never be moved — they tend to keep the house, car, dog, cat, boat, lamp, coat, pen, mate, etc., forever! The Phlegmatic quietly hoards their money and can be financial secure to everyone's surprise.

Decision Making

The Phlegmatic takes an excessive amount of time to make a decision — and sometimes they never do! They are paralyzed by their need to accommodate others and they fear their decision will not be met with approval by all involved. They put it off until forced to decide — even then it still may not happen.

Leadership Style

The Phlegmatic will manage their home and career in a low-key, non-emotional manner. They will be soft and accommodating adhering to the established rules and regulations of their environment. Because they do not have a sense of urgency, decisions usually take an excessive amount of time. Because of this, productivity may slow down in their area of responsibility.

The Phlegmatic will naturally want everyone to be accommodated. This results in stubbornly adhering to "the way we have always done it." They usually take a team approach to at home and work wanting everyone to cooperate. They will have difficulty when they need to confront someone because of their fear of conflict and tension.

Eating Habits

The Phlegmatic views food as pleasure. They enjoy eating and will exercise the least restraint of the four temperaments. It is this group that tends to be the most overweight. Their lack of self-discipline encourages poor eating habits — once they start eating it is difficult for them to stop.

Sleep

The Phlegmatic goes to sleep quickly and will sleep through the night. They need at least eight to nine hours of sleep each night. The are able to go to sleep most anywhere and easily dose off when sitting still or riding in a car.

View of Others

The theologian Ole Hallesby in his book, *Temperament & The Christian Faith*, says this about the Phlegmatic:

> The phlegmatic is especially subject to self-righteousness. His life is correct and balanced, without any great inclination toward evil. As a matter of mere convenience he keeps away from such sins as lewdness, villainy, drunkenness, and brutality. Because he is able to compromise his ideals, he has, in his own estimation, little cause for self-reproach. In fact, he considers himself considerably above the average in morality. He is usually interested in the church. This interest too is of a placid nature; he is conservative for the simple reason that this point of view requires the least exertion. To be sure, his interest in the church is neither very active nor very hearty.

The Phlegmatic does not have the anxieties of the other three temperaments. The Choleric is concerned about getting results. The Sanguine is concerned about being accepted socially. The Melancholy is concerned about knowing what is right. The Phlegmatic isn't typically concerned a great deal about any of these things. For this reason they can be sarcastic when speaking about the anxieties of the other three temperaments; this is an expression of pride, "I'm not like other people." This attitude may be well hidden and not known to others.

As a Mate

The Phlegmatic can be affectionate but it takes some time to warm up. They will resist sudden change in their established routine. This can be an issue if married to an extrovert that can change quickly. The Phlegmatic is loyal to their mate and family and they like to stay home. They make good companions because they are patient and tolerant of other people's shortcomings. They are slow to get upset and rarely show much emotion.

The Phlegmatic tends to be grudge holders. Their mate may not know that they are unhappy about something that happened years before. They are not naturally flexible, spontaneous, impulsive, or talkative (unless Sanguine is their second temperament). This requires a lot of patience from their mate. They typically do not like to be on the go or be with people other than family. The Phlegmatic is more of a spectator of life rather than a participant. They dislike tension and conflict. The Phlegmatic easily procrastinates. Their motto is "why do today what can be put off until tomorrow." These tendencies will be modified depending on the influence of the second temperament and their maturity level.

How Would a Phlegmatic Manage Their Family?

Phlegmatic individuals are typically calm, peaceful, and composed. They are often characterized by their patience, reliability, and tendency to avoid conflict. Rather than using forceful control, a Phlegmatic person tends to manage and influence their family in subtle, nurturing, and consistent ways. Here's how a Phlegmatic might navigate and influence family dynamics, the Phlegmatic will likely ...

1. ... demonstrate a calm demeanor which has a stabilizing effect on their family. In times of stress or conflict, their ability to remain level-headed and emotionally steady makes them a reliable anchor. This creates an environment where their family members may turn to them for guidance and reassurance, giving the Phlegmatic a natural, quiet authority.

2. ... avoid conflict and maintain harmony. Since Phlegmatics dislike confrontation they are good at keeping the peace. They usually avoid engaging in heated arguments or power struggles. By staying neutral and mediating disputes, they help maintain a harmonious atmosphere. This ability to prevent conflict often positions them as the "peacekeeper" within the family, giving them indirect control over how things unfold.

3. ... show empathy and active listening. Phlegmatic individuals are excellent listeners and tend to be empathetic. They listen carefully to the needs and concerns of their family members and respond in

a thoughtful, understanding way. This makes them approachable and trusted, allowing them to influence family decisions or dynamics by offering calm, rational advice that others respect.

3. ... show empathy and active listening. Phlegmatic individuals are excellent listeners and tend to be empathetic. They listen carefully to the needs and concerns of their family members and respond in a thoughtful, understanding way. This makes them approachable and trusted, allowing them to influence family decisions or dynamics by offering calm, rational advice that others respect.

4. ... be reliabile and consistent. Phlegmatics are dependable and often take on roles in the family where stability is needed. Whether it's managing household tasks or providing emotional support, their consistency ensures that things run smoothly. Because they can be counted on to fulfill their responsibilities without drama, they earn the respect of their family members, which gives them influence.

5. ... offer subtle guidance and support. Rather than asserting themselves overtly, Phlegmatics tend to guide their family members by setting an example through their calm and thoughtful actions. They don't force decisions on others, but their steady approach to life can inspire family members to follow their lead.

6. .. create a safe environment. Phlegmatic individuals often prioritize creating a peaceful and safe home environment. Their ability to stay composed in stressful situations allows them to provide a sense of security for their family. This calm environment fosters trust and emotional closeness, which gives them a form of influence over the family's emotional state.

7. ... be supportive and encouraging. Phlegmatics tend to support and encourage their family members in a non-pressuring way. They offer emotional support without being overbearing, and they provide the space for family members to grow and make decisions independently. They might not be the loudest or most commanding in the family, but their steady, supportive role allows them to influence family members through quiet encouragement.

8. ... encourage a balanced lifestyle, avoiding extreme behavior or decisions. They help maintain equilibrium in family dynamics by being a voice of reason when others may be too impulsive or emotional. Their tendency to weigh all sides of an issue carefully can make them a trusted advisor when decisions need to be made.

Concerns: Phlegmatics may struggle with asserting themselves or making decisions quickly, especially if they fear causing discomfort or conflict. Their reluctance to confront problems directly might lead to issues being swept under the rug, potentially causing them to lose influence in situations where more active and direct intervention is needed.

In Conclusion: Phlegmatics tend to control or influence their family not through dominance or authority, but through their steady, supportive, and nurturing nature. They provide a peaceful and stable foundation for the family, subtly guiding others with their calm presence, empathy, and consistency.

Proverbs 3:5-6

Trust in the Lord with all your heart,

And lean not on your own understanding;

6 In all your ways acknowledge Him,

And He shall direct your paths.

Chapter 5

The Inspector
Phlegmatic-Choleric

The Inspector is a combination of the Phlegmatic temperament being first and the Choleric temperament being second. Your primary motivation is to be *accommodating*. Your secondary motivation is to g*et results*. Either need may dominate your behavior depending on the requirements of the situation.

Inspector Pattern
As a Phlegmatic and Choleric your natural tendencies combine to produces an accommodating, loyal, result-oriented person who is unyielding in your routine at home or at work. You naturally concentrate on one thing at a time with strong determination to finish the task. Your combination of the Phlegmatic and Choleric temperament is one of the *least* found combinations.

Description
You prefer to be alone, with family, or a few close friends. You have an anchored determination to follow your routine or complete a task. You are accommodating, industrious, and independent (loner). You have a firm, stoic expression (flat affect) and will rarely smile. You are calm, steady, and persevering. You can be very blunt, stubborn, and sarcastic. You rarely show emotion or affection. You want to operate by yourself and set your own pace. Once your mind is made up you will resist any other method of approach. You seek challenging assignments without close supervision. You prefer work that is challenging rather than involvement with people. You are focused and bring a deceptively intense approach to the task at home or at work. After starting a project you are tenacious and will fight for your method. You are very independent, questioning, and thorough in your approach and will follow through to see the task completed. You can be very pushy.

You will become sleepy when sitting still after only a few minutes. You are very dependable, loyal, and routine. You are an anchor of reality. You need time to warm-up before showing some friendliness.

Strengths
As a Phlegmatic-Choleric you are dependable, determined, and not easily distracted. You are accommodating to a point, as long as it does not interfere with your routine. Once you accept a task at home or at work you are unyielding in your commitment to completing it (you rarely give up). You exhibit calmness in a crisis.

Weaknesses
Your effectiveness in relationships and productivity in your career may be hindered because of your resistance to change and bluntness. You project aloofness and lack compassion. You are possessive to

a fault and can be very stubborn if it is not your idea. You can also be indecisive and inflexible.

Mood Shift

You are first an introvert that prefers a quite, routine life with family or a few close friends. You are also partly an extrovert that can be direct, controlling, and result-orientrd. You can demonstrate both behaviors depending on what is required. The shift is a normal functioning of your temperament blend.

Needs

You will perform at your best and will be highly motivated if your natural, basic needs are met, such as: having a low-key environment, time to change your routine, and clear, specific instructions on when to start and stop a task. You need the opportunity to steadily work toward results. You are very independent and need the freedom to establish your own pace.

Fears

Fear tends to create anger. Fear is a primary emotion and anger is a secondary emotion. You may respond with anger if any of your natural fears are realized, such as: too much social involvement with people, abstract ideas, sudden change, loss of independence, and interference with family time.

Response to Pressure

When under pressure or stress you will likely withdraw and worry or may become blunt and sarcastic. You may procrastinate and take no action. You often release your frustration with an outburst of anger and/or excessive sleeping.

Causes of Procrastination

You will likely procrastinate because the activity does not fit your routine and you do not want to change — you are capable of strongly resisting change. Sometimes you procrastinate because you are not sure how to accommodate everyone involved and you are trying to avoid conflict.

You need slight and consistent pressure to be encouraged to act and sometimes a lot of pushing is needed. You need to see it is okay to act although not everyone will be accommodated. You need to consider that a change in your routine is not always undesirable.

Different Expressions of the Phlegmatic-Choleric Blend

People are infinitely complex. No two individuals will behave the same even with the same temperament blend. There are three major levels of expression listed below. These levels are fixed and do not change over a person's lifespan. What changes is whether or not a person uses their natural strengths and overcomes the negative impact of their natural weaknesses. The Phlegmatic, at all three levels, is driven to maintain a routine, resist change, and avoid conflict.

Level 1 - Narrow

This means the *influence* of the *second* temperament (Choleric) is ***not far from*** the first temperament (Sanguine): **Phlegmatic → Choleric**. The closer these two temperaments are to each other the more competition there is between the two for expression in behavior. In this alignment, the secondary Choleric traits are more observable in behavior. When *very* close, it produces a more forceful, blunt person, that can be direct, sarcastic, insensitive, and result driven.

The closeness of the Choleric tendencies will also speed up and intensify the expression of the Phlegmatic tendencies; they will *stubbornly* resist any change to their routine. They may also resist authority. They will have only a few close relationships over their lifespan.

Level 2 - Moderate
The spread between the Phlegmatic and Choleric is enough to allow the Phlegmatic tendencies to be expressed and easily seen in interaction with others: **Phlegmatic → → Choleric**. In this alignment, the softness of the Phlegmatic tendencies are more easily seen when interacting with others. The spread between the Phlegmatic and Choleric is enough to allow the Choleric tendencies to be expressed when communicating with others like being brief, direct, and mater-of-fact without emotion.

Level 3 - Wide
This means that there is a *significant* separation of the *second* temperament (Phlegmatic) from the *first* temperament (Sanguine): **Phlegmatic → → → Choleric**. In this alignment, the more the Phlegmatic is *separated* from the Choleric, the more Phlegmatic tendencies will be visible in behavior like being a little more open and showing a little more acceptance when interacting with others. This person will be less blunt and direct but can still be insensitive, cold, and sarcastic. The primary Phlegmatic temperament will be more *intensely* expressed the greater the separation from the Choleric (second) temperament.

Influence of the third and fourth temperaments:
The Phlegmatic and Choleric combination produces a *strong* resistance to influence from the Sanguine and Melancholy tendencies. There will, therefore, be only *slight* influence from these two temperaments based on their position.

A. When the **Sanguine** is third, the person will be *slightly* more friendly but less compliant due to the Melancholy being the fourth (and least) tendency. The combination of the Phlegmatic and Choleric produces a barrier that prevents the presence of the Sanguine to make a significant impact on behavior.

B. When the **Melancholy** is third, the person will be *slightly* more attentive to details but very resistant to being social due to the Sanguine being the fourth (and least) tendency. With the Sanguine being fourth, it would be very difficult for this person to show warmth in relationships.

Note: The closeness (proximity) of the *second* temperament, Choleric, to the *primary* temperament, Phlegmatic, makes the biggest difference in how this combination is expressed in normal, natural behavior.

Phlegmatic-Choleric Strengths

A. Your Evaluation

Check ✓ all that represent your behavior and rate each one on a scale of one to ten:

☐ Calmness in a crisis   Like Me 10—9—8—7—6—5—4—3—2—1 Not Like Me
☐ Dependable   Like Me 10—9—8—7—6—5—4—3—2—1 Not Like Me
☐ Determined   Like Me 10—9—8—7—6—5—4—3—2—1 Not Like Me
☐ Not easily distracted   Like Me 10—9—8—7—6—5—4—3—2—1 Not Like Me
☐ Will follow through / not give up
                                    Like Me 10—9—8—7—6—5—4—3—2—1 Not Like Me
☐ Accommodating   Like Me 10—9—8—7—6—5—4—3—2—1 Not Like Me
☐ Patient   Like Me 10—9—8—7—6—5—4—3—2—1 Not Like Me
☐ Responsible   Like Me 10—9—8—7—6—5—4—3—2—1 Not Like Me
☐ Routine   Like Me 10—9—8—7—6—5—4—3—2—1 Not Like Me

1. How aware are you of your natural strengths?

    Aware   10—9—8—7—6—5—4—3—2—1   Not Aware

2. List three strengths that you appreciate the most about yourself?

    _____

    _____

    _____

3. How can expressing these strengths in a controlled manner help you be more effective?

    _____

    _____

4. On the next page: ask someone who knows you well (mate, family member, friend, etc.) to check ✓ all that represent your behavior and ask them to rate each one on a scale of one to ten.

Phlegmatic-Choleric Strengths

B. Second Evaluation by:

Name _____ Date _____

Check ✓ all that represent the behavior of the person you are evaluating and rate each one on a scale of one to ten:

☐ Calmness in a crisis   Like Me 10—9—8—7—6—5—4—3—2—1 Not Like Me
☐ Dependable   Like Me 10—9—8—7—6—5—4—3—2—1 Not Like Me
☐ Determined   Like Me 10—9—8—7—6—5—4—3—2—1 Not Like Me
☐ Not easily distracted   Like Me 10—9—8—7—6—5—4—3—2—1 Not Like Me
☐ Will follow through / not give up   Like Me 10—9—8—7—6—5—4—3—2—1 Not Like Me
☐ Accommodating   Like Me 10—9—8—7—6—5—4—3—2—1 Not Like Me
☐ Patient   Like Me 10—9—8—7—6—5—4—3—2—1 Not Like Me
☐ Responsible   Like Me 10—9—8—7—6—5—4—3—2—1 Not Like Me

Compare the choices you made with the person that did the same. Answer the following:

1. Was the evaluation the same?   ☐ Yes ☐ No

2. Discuss the agreement or disagreement.

3. What did you learn from this exercise?

_____

4. What do you need to improve?

_____

_____

Phlegmatic-Choleric's
Positive Impact on Others

As a Phlegmatic-Choleric you have a natural, positive impact on others. Check ✓ all that apply from the following list:

☐ Determination   Like Me 10—9—8—7—6—5—4—3—2—1 Not Like Me

☐ Loyalty   Like Me 10—9—8—7—6—5—4—3—2—1 Not Like Me

☐ Consistency   Like Me 10—9—8—7—6—5—4—3—2—1 Not Like Me

☐ Dependable   Like Me 10—9—8—7—6—5—4—3—2—1 Not Like Me

☐ Practical   Like Me 10—9—8—7—6—5—4—3—2—1 Not Like Me

☐ Stability   Like Me 10—9—8—7—6—5—4—3—2—1 Not Like Me

☐ Patient   Like Me 10—9—8—7—6—5—4—3—2—1 Not Like Me

Which one has the greatest impact on others?

_____

Which one do you need to use/develop more?

_____

How will you use/develop the one you chose?

_____

_____

_____

_____

Phlegmatic-Choleric Weaknesses

A. Your Evaluation

☐ Blunt   Like Me 10—9—8—7—6—5—4—3—2—1 Not Like Me

☐ Stubborn   Like Me 10—9—8—7—6—5—4—3—2—1 Not Like Me

☐ Resists change   Like Me 10—9—8—7—6—5—4—3—2—1 Not Like Me

☐ Sarcastic   Like Me 10—9—8—7—6—5—4—3—2—1 Not Like Me

☐ Indecisive   Like Me 10—9—8—7—6—5—4—3—2—1 Not Like Me

☐ Aloof   Like Me 10—9—8—7—6—5—4—3—2—1 Not Like Me

☐ Overlooks details   Like Me 10—9—8—7—6—5—4—3—2—1 Not Like Me

☐ Cold   Like Me 10—9—8—7—6—5—4—3—2—1 Not Like Me

☐ Lacks compassion   Like Me 10—9—8—7—6—5—4—3—2—1 Not Like Me

☐ Possessive   Like Me 10—9—8—7—6—5—4—3—2—1 Not Like Me

1. How aware are you of these natural weaknesses?

    Aware   10—9—8—7—6—5—4—3—2—1   Not Aware

2. List one weakness that you would like to overcome.

    _____

3. How does this weakness interfere with your effectiveness in your daily life?

    _____

4. How would your relationships improve if you developed a plan to control and overcome the negative impact of your weaknesses?

    ☐ I would be more effective   ☐ Stress will be reduced

    ☐ I would be better received by others   ☐ Communication with others will improve

5. On the next page: ask someone who knows you well (mate, family member, friend, etc.) to check all that represent your behavior and ask them to rate each one on a scale of one to ten.

Phlegmatic-Choleric Weaknesses

B. Second Evaluation by:

Name _____ Date _____

Check ✓ all that represent the behavior of the person you are evaluating and rate each one on a scale of one to ten:

☐ Blunt   Like Me 10—9—8—7—6—5—4—3—2—1 Not Like Me

☐ Stubborn   Like Me 10—9—8—7—6—5—4—3—2—1 Not Like Me

☐ Resists change   Like Me 10—9—8—7—6—5—4—3—2—1 Not Like Me

☐ Sarcastic   Like Me 10—9—8—7—6—5—4—3—2—1 Not Like Me

☐ Indecisive   Like Me 10—9—8—7—6—5—4—3—2—1 Not Like Me

☐ Aloof   Like Me 10—9—8—7—6—5—4—3—2—1 Not Like Me

☐ Overlooks details   Like Me 10—9—8—7—6—5—4—3—2—1 Not Like Me

☐ Cold   Like Me 10—9—8—7—6—5—4—3—2—1 Not Like Me

☐ Lacks compassion   Like Me 10—9—8—7—6—5—4—3—2—1 Not Like Me

☐ Possessive   Like Me 10—9—8—7—6—5—4—3—2—1 Not Like Me

Compare the choices you make with the person that did the same. Answer the following:

1. Was agreement close to the same?   ☐ Yes ☐ No
2. Discuss the differences if any.
3. What did you learn from this exercise?

_____

_____

_____

_____

How To Deal With Weaknesses

All temperament blends have *natural* strengths and weaknesses. However, a strength overextended will become a weakness. Your lack of self-control will cause the weaknesses listed above.

To overcome any weakness you must first become ***aware*** that it is something you do, take ***ownership*** of what you are doing, and then ***decide*** to ***change*** your thinking and behavior.

>**Romans 12:2** *And do not be conformed to this world, but be transformed by the renewing of your mind* (see page 53-54).

•*Change Your Thinking.* This passage teaches that you have to *change* what you have been thinking and doing. You do that by *renewing* your mind. The word *renewing* means to *renovate* (when you renovate something you take out old and replace it with new). So, when you *renovate* your mind you take out *old* thinking and behavior and replace it with *new* thinking and behavior. The old thinking and behavior that shows weaknesses has to *stop* and be replaced with *new* thinking and behavior that comes from the Bible.

•*Use Self-Control.* Once the decision is made to change you now must engage in redirecting or re-programming your thoughts, feelings, and behavior by using self-control. Every book in the New Testament includes instructions like *put on, put off, start, stop.* All the writers encouraged self-control to *stop* certain behavior and start better behavior. This is a process that takes time to gain mastery over your thoughts, feelings, behavior, desires, speech, and impulses (see pages 55-58).

>**Ephesians 4:22-24** *that you **put off**, concerning your former conduct, the old man which grows corrupt according to the deceitful lusts, 23 and be renewed in the spirit of your mind, 24 and that you **put on** the new man which was created according to God, in true righteousness and holiness.*

>**Galatians 5:22-23** *But the fruit of the Spirit is love, joy, peace, longsuffering, kindness, goodness, faithfulness, gentleness, **self-control**.*

>**Proverbs 16:32** *Better a patient person than a warrior, one with **self-control** than one who takes a city.*

The contrast in Proverbs 16:32 is between having great *physical strength* verses having *self-control*. First, you are far better to be patient (slow to anger) than one who is physically very strong. Second, if you control your spirit or temper, you are better than one who can capture a city. The idea is that you are so physically strong that you not only *capture* a city but you alone can *keep* the city under your control!

Issues you may struggle with are listed below with suggestions on how to overcome the negative impact they may be having in your life.

1. Resists change. As a Phlegmatic you find security in a routine making it difficult to change behavior to align with Scripture. Romans 12:2 quoted above requires a change in the way you think and behave to grow spiritually.

      ☐ I am willing to change.

2. **Anxiety.** As a Phlegmatic you tend to worry about most anything especially family members. When you worry you are leaving God out of the situation. **Philippines 4:6-7** (see pages 67-68)

> *Be anxious for nothing, but in everything by prayer and supplication, with thanksgiving, let your requests be made known to God; 7 and the peace of God, which surpasses all understanding, will guard your hearts and minds through Christ Jesus.*

      ☐ I choose to trust God and not be anxious.

3. **Resentment.** When you end a relationship it is highly unlikely for it to be restored (of course, sometimes it's appropriate to end a relationship). Consider, however, if you need to forgive the person for the grievance. **Ephesians 4:31-32:**

> *31 Let all bitterness, wrath, anger, clamor, and evil speaking be put away from you, with all malice. 32 And be kind to one another, tenderhearted, forgiving one another, even as God in Christ forgave you.*

      ☐ I am willing to forgive.

4. **Sarcastic and Blunt.** Be aware that your tone of voice may have a *bite* in it. Having a *bite* means that you can show *irritation* in the way you are speaking. The *bite* represents anger and discuss. Love doesn't act this way. Here are a few ways that love behaves. **I Corinthians 13:4-8** (for a full list see pages 77-78):

•Love is patient - love never takes the opportunity to avenge itself.
•Love is kind - love never offends, insults or says anything unkind.
•Love is not rude - love has good manners and makes you feel comfortable.
•Love seeks not it's own - love does not trade being right for another person's feelings.
•Love is not provoked - love does not get irritated.

A Summary of I Corinthians 13:4-8 by Dr. Tom Constable:
Love does not deal with other people in a way that injures their dignity. It does not insist on having its own way, nor does it put its own interest before the needs of others. Love is not irritable or touchy, and it **absorbs** offenses, insults, and inconveniences for the sake of others' welfare. It does not keep a record of offenses received to pay them back.

      ☐ I will love others like this.

5. **Lacks compassion.** Put yourself in the other person's shoes. Understand what they are feeling and why. **I Peter 3:8:**

> *Finally, all of you be of one mind, having **compassion** for one another; love as brothers, be tenderhearted, be courteous;*

☐ I will form the habit of understanding what others might be feeling.

6. **Self-control.** Every book in the New Testament includes instructions to *put on, put off, start, stop.* All the writers encouraged self-control to *stop* certain behavior and start better behavior (see pages 57-60)..

For example, if you overlook details, stop it, start giving attention to details. Form a new habit. If you lack a sense of urgency, stop procrastinating, start doing things more quickly. Form a new habit.

> **Ephesians 4:22-24** *that you put off, concerning your former conduct, the old man which grows corrupt according to the deceitful lusts, 23 and be renewed in the spirit of your mind, 24 and that you put on the new man which was created according to, God in true righteousness and holiness.*

> **Proverbs 25:28** *Whoever has no rule over his own spirit is like a city broken down, without walls.*

☐ I will start forming better habits.

How To Deal With Fears

The first negative emotion experience by Adam and Eve was the fear that God would find out what they had done, Genesis 3:8-10. Now, everyone is fearful of something, for example, anyone may fear harm, loss, death, etc. Here are some fears often associated with the Phlegmatic-Choleric temperament, you may fear...

    1. <u>Giving Feedback to Others</u>. Sometimes family members, friends, or co-workers you believe need to have something pointed out that needs to be corrected. But the slightest form of conflict makes you uncomfortable, so you will try to avoid it if possible.

    Love is the primary reason to offer feedback to others. Love defined means to "seek the highest good for another person." Feedback is, therefore, an act of love. When you know you should offer feedback and do not, you are acting in your best interest. Lack of feedback is, therefore, selfishness. You may be attempting to avoid conflict, rejection, or embarrassment which may be good for you at the moment. But, in so doing you may fail to help the one who needs your counsel.

    2. <u>Other Fears</u>. As mention before, typical fears include the fear of dishamony, change, loss of routine, loss of freedom, too much involvement with people, infringement on home life, and expressing feelings or emotions.

Deal with fear Biblically.

Christians are commanded not to fear throughout the Bible. Actually it is the most repeated command in the Bible. There are at least 365 occurrences of fear not in the Bible, one for each day!

    God wants you to want what He wants. God wants you be willing to accept the outcome of anything you are trying to do as coming from Him. When you fear that you will not get what you want you are bypassing what God is doing in your life.

    The purpose of the Christian life is to be conformed into the image of His Son. So, all things that happen in your life have a purpose, even experiencing losing, or having to be in a fixed environment. This means that God doesn't do anything **to** you, He does it **for** you (see page 51).

> Romans 8:28-29 And we know that all things work together for good to those who love God, to those who are the called according to His purpose. 29 For whom He foreknew, He also predestined to be conformed to the image of His Son, that He might be the firstborn among many brethren.
> *among many brethren.*

Guidelines to help you face and overcome fear:

A. <u>Acknowledge God's presence</u>. The Bible reminds us that we are never alone, and God is always with us. When fear arises, remember that God's presence is with you, and He will give you the strength to face any challenge.

Isaiah 41:10 *So do not fear, for I am with you; do not be dismayed, for I am your God. I will strengthen you and help you; I will uphold you with my righteous right hand.*

B. <u>Trust in God's sovereignty</u>. Understanding that God is in control of all circumstances can help relieve fear. Fear stems from a sense of uncertainty but knowing that God is sovereign reassures us that He is in control.

Psalm 34:4 *I sought the Lord, and he answered me; he delivered me from all my fears.*

Romans 8:28 *And we know that in all things God works for the good of those who love him, who have been called according to his purpose.*

1 Thessalonians 5:18 *in everything give thanks; for this is the will of God in Christ Jesus for you.*

Trust that no matter what happens, God is working for your good.

C. <u>Cast your cares on God</u>. Instead of letting fear control you, take your concerns directly to God in prayer. He cares for you and wants to carry your burdens. This act of surrender helps release the grip of fear and anxiety.

1 Peter 5:7 *Cast all your anxiety on him because he cares for you.*

D. <u>Change your thinking.</u> Change from "I am afraid" to I am not afraid." I know that's not so easy to do so the next time you are fearful of something quote **Proverbs 3:5-6:**

Trust in the Lord with all your heart, And lean not on your own understanding; 6 In all your ways acknowledge Him, And He shall direct your paths.

Do not leave God out of what is happening. Thank God for using the event to help conform you into Christ's image. Check ✓ what you will do to overcome the negative impact fear is having in your life:

☐ I will not be fearful of what may or may not happen.

☐ I will trust God no matter what happens.

Phlegmatic-Choleric Tendencies Needed For Balance

In order to be a more balanced person, as a Phlegmatic-Choleric, you need to incorporate tendencies from both the Sanguine and Melancholy temperaments into your behavior.

To this point, the focus has been on the primary and the secondary temperaments that make up your temperament combination. You are, however, a blend of all four temperaments. You can be either Phlegmatic-Choleric-**Sanguine**-Melancholy or Phlegmatic-Choleric-**Melancholy** -Sanguine. A common blend is the Melancholy being third. The influence of either of these on your blend is minimal.

Regardless of the natural position of the Phlegmatic and Melancholy temperaments become comfortable with expressing either tendency when the need arises. Adding the tendencies of the third and fourth temperaments will enable you to have a balanced approach to dealing with others and the circumstances of life.

Check ✓ all the needs below that you feel would complement your temperament combination and is lacking in your behavior. Rate your level of need on a scale of one to ten:

☐ Be more sensitive   Needed 10—9—8—7—6—5—4—3—2—1 Not needed

☐ Use gentle tone when speaking to others   Needed 10—9—8—7—6—5—4—3—2—1 Not needed

☐ More attention to details   Needed 10—9—8—7—6—5—4—3—2—1 Not needed

☐ More social involvement   Needed 10—9—8—7—6—5—4—3—2—1 Not needed

☐ More openness   Needed 10—9—8—7—6—5—4—3—2—1 Not needed

☐ Self-control   Needed 10—9—8—7—6—5—4—3—2—1 Not needed

☐ Compassion   Needed 10—9—8—7—6—5—4—3—2—1 Not needed

The four temperaments represent *different* ways of approaching people and events. In a given situation a tendency from another temperament may be more effective and efficient. The key is to be flexible and willing to function in any of the four temperament tendencies when it is necessary.

For example, as a Phlegmatic-Choleric, you are likely to overlook careful planning, whereas, the Melancholy tendency is to plan carefully. Choose to operate from a plan. As a Phlegmatic-Choleric you may avoid being around others socially. Whereas the Sanguine tendency is to be around others to socialize. Choose to be more social. Adding these two tendencies to your behavior will make you a more effective person.

       ☐ I choose to plan more.

       ☐ I choose to be social.

Questions For Reflection and Growth

1. Which one did you select that needs the most attention now and what will you do?

_____

_____

_____

1. Write down the problems that have occurred because of a lack of these tendencies in your daily behavior. Be specific and brief.

_____

_____

_____

2. Now write out the reasons why you should practice these tendencies. How will it help you to become a more balanced person? Be specific and brief.

_____

_____

_____

3. Write out how you will incorporate these characteristics into your daily behavior. Be specific and brief.

_____

_____

_____

Phlegmatic-Choleric Needs

Select 10 of the following temperament needs:

CHECK ✓ ONLY 10

1. ☐ I need a plan.
2. ☐ I need to have fun.
3. ☐ I need to be led gently, don't push on me.
4. ☐ I need feedback.
5. ☐ I need brief and direct answers.

6. ☐ I need to know the big picture.
7. ☐ I need to know I'm appreciated.
8. ☐ I need freedom from details.
9. ☐ I need low key correction.
10. ☐ I need to tell people what to do.

11. ☐ I need time to think.
12. ☐ I need to learn by doing.
13. ☐ I need to have frequent talks.
14. ☐ I need to be by myself when bothered.
15. ☐ I need social involvement with my friends.

16. ☐ I need tolerance when I get aggressive.
17. ☐ I need to know why.
18. ☐ I need you to *show* me first then *tell* me how.
19. ☐ I need the freedom to talk.
20. ☐ I need to ask questions.

21. ☐ I need a stable environment.
22. ☐ I need you to not hang over my shoulder.
23. ☐ I need help so I will not seek perfection.
24. ☐ I need facts logically given.
25. ☐ I need you to get to the point.

26. ☐ I need help organizing.
27. ☐ I need to say it only once.
28. ☐ I need to talk about what's bothering me.
29. ☐ I need time to adjust to change.
30. ☐ I need to know the results expected.

31. ☐ I need to know exactly what is expected of me.
32. ☐ I need reassurance that I'm doing the job right.
33. ☐ I need a flexible schedule.
34. ☐ I need information.
35. ☐ I need help handling rejection.

36. ☐ I need you to help me say "no."
37. ☐ I need you to tell me only once.
38. ☐ I need you to help me do things *right*.
39. ☐ I need social activity.
40. ☐ I need you to help me get results quickly.

Write down the ten needs you selected and their number **in order of their importance**. Which one is the most important, which one is the next important, etc. Also, rate how well each need is being met on a scale of one to ten.

For example: #17   I need to know why.

How well is this need being met?   10—9—(8)—7—6—5—4—3—2—1

1. #____   _____

How well is this need being met?   10—9—8—7—6—5—4—3—2—1

2. #____   _____

How well is this need being met?   10—9—8—7—6—5—4—3—2—1

3. #____   _____

How well is this need being met?   10—9—8—7—6—5—4—3—2—1

4. #____   _____

How well is this need being met?   10—9—8—7—6—5—4—3—2—1

5. #____   _____

How well is this need being met?   10—9—8—7—6—5—4—3—2—1

6. #____   _____

How well is this need being met?   10—9—8—7—6—5—4—3—2—1

7. #____   _____

How well is this need being met?   10—9—8—7—6—5—4—3—2—1

8. #____   _____

How well is this need being met?   10—9—8—7—6—5—4—3—2—1

9. #____   _____

How well is this need being met?   10—9—8—7—6—5—4—3—2—1

10. #____   _____

How well is this need being met?   10—9—8—7—6—5—4—3—2—1

Questions For Reflection and Growth

1. Answer the following questions:

    Is your most important need being met?   ☐ Yes ☐ No

    If "No," complete the following:

2. Write out how you will incorporate this need into your daily behavior. Be specific and brief.

    _____

    _____

3. Which needs are not being met? What can you change to meet these needs?

    _____

    _____

    _____

    _____

    _____

    _____

    _____

    _____

4. How can you lovingly share those needs with those who are important to you?

    _____

    _____

5. Select one that needs the most attention now and what will you do?

    _____

    _____

    _____

6. Write down the problems that have occurred because of a lack of these tendencies in your daily behavior. Be specific and brief.

    _____

    _____

    _____

7. Now write out the reasons why you should practice these tendencies. How will it help you to become a more balanced person? Be specific and brief.

    _____

    _____

    _____

8. Write out how you will incorporate these characteristics into your daily behavior. Be specific and brief.

    _____

    _____

    _____

Phlegmatic-Choleric
Responses Needed From Others

You prefer other people to respond to you a certain way. Check ✓ all that you would like others to do for you:

☐ I would like others to understand my need for a routine.

      Needed 10—9—8—7—6—5—4—3—2—1 Not needed

☐ I would like others to tell me clearly what is expected.

      Needed 10—9—8—7—6—5—4—3—2—1 Not needed

☐ I would like others to give me specific instructions.

      Needed 10—9—8—7—6—5—4—3—2—1 Not needed

☐ I would like others help me to be more organized.

      Needed 10—9—8—7—6—5—4—3—2—1 Not needed

☐ I would like others to help me develop more compassion and show more affection.

      Needed 10—9—8—7—6—5—4—3—2—1 Not needed

☐ I would like others to not push me.

      Needed 10—9—8—7—6—5—4—3—2—1 Not needed

Be careful with whom (and how) you share these request. It's meant to be shared with family and friends and if you hold a position of authority, those under your supervision. Don't demand that others do theses things, just explain that this is your preferred way to be treated and you will do the same for them. This will help you develop patience. See the next page for *effective responses* and follow these rules:

**If I meet the needs of your temperament it will increase
the possibility of a favorable response.**

**The way people communicate with you
is the way they want you to communicate with them.**

Phlegmatic-Choleric's Environment Needed

As a Phlegmatic-Choleric you function best in an environment that meets your temperament needs. Make careful, responsible choices, that provide the best environment for you to flourish and be at your best.

Check ✓ all of those that represent a preferred environment and rate each on a scale of one to ten:

☐ Clear plan to follow   Needed 10—9—8—7—6—5—4—3—2—1 Not needed

☐ Specific instructions   Needed 10—9—8—7—6—5—4—3—2—1 Not needed

☐ Routine   Needed 10—9—8—7—6—5—4—3—2—1 Not needed

☐ Time to change my routine   Needed 10—9—8—7—6—5—4—3—2—1 Not needed

☐ Opportunity to work alone   Needed 10—9—8—7—6—5—4—3—2—1 Not needed

☐ Opportunity to get results   Needed 10—9—8—7—6—5—4—3—2—1 Not needed

1. Are you in an environment that best fits your temperament needs?   ☐ Yes ☐ No

2. What can you do to improve your environment?

_____

_____

_____

_____

_____

Effective Responses

For the Choleric:

•Be brief, to the point.

•Be direct.

•Be confident.

•Give them facts.

•Be result oriented.

•Be practical.

•Help them save time.

•Be objective, matter-of-fact.

•Discuss getting better, faster results.

•Tolerate their assertive, forceful responses, and their crisis style of communication.

For the Sanguine:

•Be friendly and open.

•Build the relationship.

•Be personal.

•Be willing to listen.

•Never embarrass them.

•Spend informal time with them.

•Provide them with details.

•Remind them often, they easily forget.

•Be open about self, feelings, opinions.

•Tolerate their impulsiveness and need to talk.

For the Phlegmatic:

•Be warm and personal.

•Show interest in family.

•Use visual aids.

•Have a slow pace.

•Never hurry a conversation.

•Be in control of your emotions.

•Be willing to repeat information.

•Avoid asking for sudden change.

•Tell them you "sincerely" appreciate efforts.

•Tolerate their slow pace and lack of a sense of urgency.

For the Melancholy:

•Be considerate and personal.

•Allow time for research.

•Give reassurance.

•Give feedback.

•Give lots of information.

•Listen carefully to their ideas.

•Be specific, factual and logical.

•Discuss what is "right" or "best."

•Give specific, detailed, instructions.

•Tolerate their need to check for accuracy and time to think about a proposal.

PART III

Biblical Principles To Practice For Spiritual Growth

If you are **angry**
you're living in the past.

If you are **anxious**
you're living in the future.

If you are **depressed** you're
thinking about the wrong thing.

If you have **peace**
you're living in the present
and trusting God.

Chapter 6

Introduction to Living the Spiritual Life

Why this section? Every Christian, regardless of their temperament blend, struggles with the issues that will be discussed. Disobedience isn't reserved to a specific temperament. All Christians have the same problem, we disobey God. For example, the four temperaments all have an issue with anger, but for different reasons. The Choleric will likely show anger because a goal was not accomplished, a Sanguine may show anger if they are embarrassed in public, the Phlegmatic may show anger if their routine is interrupted, and the Melancholy may show anger if they think an injustice has been done. So, all Christians need to work on not being angry regardless of the reason.

Of course, living the spiritual life is not easy. It is a process of growth that last a life time. To live as God wants us to requires unlearning patterns of thinking, feeling, and behaving that do not represent what the Bible teaches. We have to replace those patterns of thinking and behaving with how God says we should think and behave ... and that takes time.

Learning about your natural temperament tendencies and how to use and overcome the negative impact on yourself and others is a start. Next, practice the following Biblical principles daily:

1. The Purpose of The Christian Life
2. Trust God No Matter What
3. Renovate Your Thinking
4. How To Develop Self-Control
5. How To Deal With Frustration
6. Do Not Be Anxious.
7. Do Not Get Angry
8. Do Not Argue
9. Two Kinds of Guilt
10. The Cause and Cure of Depression
11. How Love Behaves
12. How to Treat People

The Scripture is very clear. It is not enough to know what God has said, you have to do what God has said. James 1:22 But be doers of the word, and not hearers only, deceiving yourselves.

If you only know what God says, and do not do it, you are deceived. What's the deception? The deception is believing that just knowing is enough! But God wants you to be a doer. The Greek word for doer means to be a performer, so you are to perform His Word. Also, the word doer is in the present tense which means you are to continually do His Word. The Greek word for deceive means you are guilty of false reasoning. So if you know the Word and do not do the Word you have reasoned incorrectly. God wants you to put the Word into practice and perform it to your life daily.

The process for this to happen is to first become aware of what you need to do, then accept ownership of what you need to do, and then actually change your thinking and behavior to do what God says.

Overcomers Will be Rewarded

To grow spiritually you must decide to use *self-control* to overcome sin as discussed throughout Scripture. This is not an easy process nor does it happen quickly. If you overcome you will live a life that is pleasing to the Lord. Remember that God will always be there to help you; Psalm 23 and Philippians 4:13. You not only will be *transformed* into Christ likeness but you will be rewarded for a life well lived. The following is from my brother Mike's book *How God Treats People*:

> According to 1 John 5:4 all believers are *overcomers*, but the present tense in the very next verse (1 Jn. 5:5) indicates that believers who continue are *overcomers*. In the book of Revelation, faithful believers are *overcomers* (Rev. 2:26).
>
> The point of the Lord telling the seven churches of Revelation about the *overcomer* getting a reward is to motivate them to live in such a way as they will receive the reward at the Judgment Seat of Christ. Do not be overcome; become an *overcomer*. In short, the *overcomer* is the believer who is rewarded for being a spiritual victor over circumstances in this life and not a victim of them.
>
> What must believers do to receive an additional inheritance? The meek shall inherit the earth (Mt. 5:5), that is, the meek, "those who do not demand their own rights, will have a special place of rule in the kingdom" (Wall, p. 83). The righteous, who help the needy, will inherit the kingdom (Mt. 25:34). Believers who are rich in faith are heirs of the kingdom (Jas. 2:5). Those who bless others will inherit a blessing (1 Pet. 3:9). Believers who suffer for Christ will be a joint-heir with Christ (Rom. 8:17). Those who heed what they have heard (Heb. 2:1) will inherit "eschatological salvation" (Heb. 1:14). Those who have faith and patience inherit the promises (Heb. 6:12, 14). The *overcomer* will inherit all things (Rev. 21:7).

Think Biblically

James 1:22 But be doers of the word, and not hearers only, deceiving yourselves.

The rest of this section has Biblical principles that will help you grow spiritually ... if you apply them to your life daily. Remember, obeying what God has said will result in you being transformed into the *likeness of Christ* and you will receive an award as an *overcomer*.

1. The Purpose of The Christian Life

Romans 8:28-29

28 And we know that all things work together for good to those who love God, to those who are the called according to His purpose. 29 For whom He foreknew, He also predestined to be conformed to the image of His Son, that He might be the firstborn among many brethren.

For the Christian, there are two ways to look at what happens in your life. You are either a victim of your circumstances or there is divine purpose involved.

God's divine purpose for life's events is identified in Romans 8:28-29. The passage states that all things work together for good. It does not say some, many, or most things work together, but all things. The accident, the lost relationship, the failed marriage, the rebellious child, the lost job, illness, financial crisis, scratching your favorite shoes, the fire, being betrayed by a family member or friend, failing to accomplish a goal, etc. I cannot possible mentioned everything someone may go through in life but you get the idea. All things, yes everything, that happens in your life can be used by God to conform you into the image of His Son, no exceptions! This means that...

God doesn't do anything TO you, He does it FOR you.

This is why you are not a victim of your circumstances. God will use anything and everything to help conform you into the image of His Son!

Now notice, the passage does not say that all things are good or that God causes all things. It says that all things are being used for good. The Greek word for good includes in the definition the idea of benefit. So all the events in your life have benefit in conforming you into the image of His Son. Of course, you may not see the benefit when the event occurs but have faith that God will somehow use the events and people to accomplish the goal of conforming you into a likeness of His Son.

This is what it means to walk by faith; you may not see how the event will be beneficial but God does. Trust God that He knows what He is doing in your past, current, and future circumstances.

The former coach of the Dallas Cowboys Tom Landry (1924-2000) was reported to have said, "We learn out of our failures not out of our successes." Imagine if your life went smoothly and you were able to get everything you wanted when you wanted it, and you had plenty of money, you never got sick, and your family and friends prospered. Would you need God for anything? The ups and downs of life are designed to get your attention so you will let God conform you into His image.

Think Biblically

Everything that happens in my life is used by God to help me
become conformed into the image of Jesus Christ.

2. Trust God No Matter What

Proverbs 3:5-6

Trust in the Lord with all your heart, And lean not on your own understanding;
6 In all your ways acknowledge Him, And He shall direct your paths.

That's right, God wants you to trust Him no matter what is happening in your life. Notice the contrast in verse 6 is between **trusting the Lord** and **trusting *your* understanding**. If we trust the Lord, we cannot *also* depend upon our reasoning to understand what God is doing. Many times we cannot make sense out of it.

Sumner Wemp, my spiritual grandfather, said to me, that Proverbs 3:5-6 is teaching us "Don't try to figure it out."

Just trust that the Lord knows what He is doing. Do not forget that it is God Who is directing your life. It is God Who determines what is best for you. It is God Who has the final decision. Not you, it is God Who sees the whole picture while we see only a tiny piece. Someone put it this way;

> To trust in the Lord with all our heart means we can't place our own right to understand above His right to direct our lives the way He sees fit. When we insist on God always making sense to our finite minds, we are setting ourselves up for spiritual trouble.

My brother, Mike, made this comment on Proverbs 3:5-6:

> The Hebrew word for "direct" means "smooth, straight, right." Smooth is being free from obstacles. These verses are not promising daily direction in all the decisions we make. They are saying that if we follow the Lord, He will make our lives go straight in the sense of righteousness, smooth in the sense of removing all hindrances out of the way.

Our limited understanding can easily lead us down the wrong path. Just trust that the Lord knows what He is doing in your life.

> Joshua 1:9 Have I not commanded you? Be strong and of good courage; do not be afraid, nor be dismayed, for the Lord your God is with you wherever you go.

> Isaiah 41:10 Fear not, for I am with you; Be not dismayed, for I am your God. I will strengthen you, Yes, I will help you, I will uphold you with My righteous right hand.

> Matthew 6:26-27 Look at the birds of the air; they do not sow or reap or store away in barns, and yet your heavenly Father feeds them. Are you not much more valuable than they? Can any one of you by worrying add a single hour to your life?

John 14:1 *Do not let your hearts be troubled. You believe in God; believe also in Me.*

Psalm 27:14 *Wait on the Lord; Be of good courage, And He shall strengthen your heart; Wait, I say, on the Lord*!

Think Biblically

Make this a part of what you think:

I will trust God no matter what happens in my life.

Remember:

God doesn't do anything **TO** me, He does it **FOR** me.

3. Renovate Your Thinking

Romans 12:1-2

I beseech you therefore, brethren, by the mercies of God, that you present your bodies a living sacrifice, holy, acceptable to God, which is your reasonable service. 2 And do not be conformed to this world, but be transformed by the renewing of your mind, that you may prove what is that good and acceptable and perfect will of God.

This passage teaches that in order for change to occur in your behavior you have to change what you have been thinking. To understand the flow of this passage I've isolated the main thoughts in verses 1 and 2 as follows:

I beseech you therefore, brethren, by the mercies of God, that you present your bodies a living sacrifice, holy, acceptable to God, which is your reasonable service.

Romans chapter 12:1 marks a turning point in the epistle. Paul uses the term *therefore* which means he has made a point in previous chapters and now he is going to apply what he has said. For example, Paul has said that because we have been *justified by faith, we have peace with God* (5:1). *I beseech you therefore* ... Paul strongly encourages (beseech is not a command) us to give ourselves as a *living sacrifice* to Him. It's only *reasonable*, the Greek word means *logical, s*o, it's *logical* for us to give back to Him *ourselves* as a *living sacrifice*. How then do we do that?

do not be conformed to his world

First, in verse 2 Paul instructs us to *not be conformed to this world.* The word *conformed* means simply *to be like.* There are two words in the Greek New Testament translated *world*. One is *cosmos* which means *universe.* The other word is *aion* which means *age.* The word used in verse 2 is *aion.* So Paul is saying that we are not *to be like* the *age* in which we live.

but be transformed

You are to be *transformed by the renewing of your mind*. Transformation is the process we are to go through in order to change. The word *transformation* appears only twice in the New Testament; Romans 12:2 and 2 Corinthians 3:18. You will recognize the Greek word translated "transform" is *metamorphoo* from which we get the word *metamorphosis*. According to Strong's Hebrew and Greek Dictionary, this Greek word means *to change to a different pattern, to change into a wholly different form or appearance.*

God has given us an example of *transformation* in nature. Every butterfly begins life as a caterpillar, goes through a *transformation,* and becomes a completely different life form. This is what every believer is to experience in their spiritual growth. It will happen when you practice daily doing what God has said.

I need to get technical to communicate an important truth. The Greek word for transformation (metamorphoo) is a verb that is in the present, passive, imperative form. All that means this: present means this is an ongoing action. The passive imperative is a command directed to you in which you are not the active doer, but rather the cooperator and recipient of someone else's doing, and yet you still retain responsibility.

So, transformation (change) happens to you. **You do not do the changing**, you receive the change. You are continually responsible to do something (mentioned next) and then change will occur. What are you supposed to do continually?

by the renewing of your mind

The meaning of the word renew holds the secret as to what anyone must do to change. The word renew means to renovate. Now what happens when you renovate something? You take out the old and put in the new!

> Remodeling a house illustrates renovation. A designer and contractor will take a used, often old home, and make it look brand new. To achieve the makeover they will take out the old fixtures, and sometimes walls, and replace the old fixtures with new ones. When finished it's impossible to see the condition it was once in.

The same process is necessary for you to change. According to Thayer's Greek-English Lexicon of The New Testament, **the meaning of the Greek word for mind (nous) includes** thoughts, feelings, purposes, and desires. So what needs to change is the way you are dealing with people and life situations.

Common issues include; anxiety, fear, frustration, irritation, anger, arguing, depression, guilt, lack of forgiveness, addictions, etc. Here's the idea. If you do any of these things it's because you think it's okay. To be transformed you must choose to think that these things are not okay.

Think Biblically: Do it God's way. Change the way you have been thinking and practice the things that are discussed in this workbook.

4. How To Develop Self-Control

Self-control is a virtue that reflects spiritual growth and maturity. It's so important that (as mentioned) every book in the New Testament has instructions to *put on, put off, start, stop.* All the writers encouraged Christians to *stop* bad behavior and *start* Godly behavior.

1. The Greek word for *self-control* (translated *temperance*) as found in Galatians 5:23, 2 Pet. 1:6, and Titus 1:8 is defined (by Thayer's Greek Definitions) "as one who masters his desires and passions, especially his sensual appetites, mastering, controlling, curbing, restraining, controlling one's self, temperate, continent."

What is it about *self* that needs controlling? You need to control what you *think*, what you *feel*, what you *do*, and what you *say*.

To achieve self-control you need to change your thinking to align with what God wants you think, feel, do, and say. Note the following passages:

Control your thoughts. 1 Peter. 1:13 Peter says, *Therefore gird up the loins of your mind, be sober, and rest your hope fully upon the grace that is to be brought to you at the revelation of Jesus Christ.* The word "self-control" does not appear in this passage but the idea is clearly there. The way to control the mind is by thinking about something else. Paul says in Philippians. 4:8 *Finally, brethren, whatever things are true, whatever things are noble, whatever things are just, whatever things are pure, whatever things are lovely, whatever things are of good report, if there is any virtue and if there is anything praiseworthy — meditate on these things.*

Control your emotions. Ephesians. 4:31-32 *Let all bitterness, wrath, anger, clamor, and evil speaking be put away from you, with all malice. And be kind to one another, tenderhearted, forgiving one another, just as God in Christ forgave you.* Again, the word self-control does not appear, but the concept is present.

Control your behavior. Proverbs 4:23-27 *Keep* [guard] *your heart with all diligence, For out of it spring the issues* [boundaries] *of life. Guard what you say. 24 Put away from you a deceitful mouth, And put perverse lips far from you. Guard what you say. 25 Let your eyes look straight ahead, And your eyelids look right before you. Guard where you go. 26 Ponder the path of your feet, And let all your ways be established. 27 Do not turn to the right or the left; Remove your foot from evil.*

Control your speech. Ephesians 4: 29 *Let no corrupt word proceed out of your mouth, but what is good for necessary edification, that it may impart grace to the hearers.*

Control your sexual desires. 1 Corinthians 6:18-20 *Flee sexual immorality. Every sin that a man does is outside the body, but he who commits sexual immorality sins against his own body. 19 Or do you not know that your body is the temple of the Holy Spirit who is in you, whom you have from God, and you are not your own? 20 For you were bought at a price; therefore glorify God in your body and in your spirit, which are God's.*

2. To develop self-control requires the following:

Impulse control: The choice to resist the urge to engage in behaviors that are impulsive or rewarding at the moment.

Delayed gratification: The choice to wait for a more valuable reward in the future rather than opting for an immediate, lesser reward.

Emotional regulation: The choice to maintain composure under stress and not react with extreme emotions.

Cognitive control: The choice to control your thoughts to stay focused on tasks, resist distractions, and manage stress or frustration.

Behavioral inhibition: The choice to not engage in undesirable behaviors.

Each temperament blend has its own challenges and struggles that differ from the other temperament blends. Your challenges to gaining self-control are, in part, related to the weaknesses mentioned earlier in this workbook. Regardless of one's temperament we are all required to gain self-control.

3. What does the Bible say about one who does not have self-control?

Proverbs 16:32 *Better a patient person than a warrior, those with self-control than those who take a city.*

Proverbs 25:28 *Like a city whose walls are broken through is a person who lacks self-control.*

James 1:6-8 in part states ... *he is a double-minded man, unstable in all his ways.*

Lacking self-control leads to instability, vulnerability, and being unstable in all your ways. One who lacks self-control cannot grow to spiritual maturity.

4. What does the Bible say about one who has self-control? Self-control produces contentment. Cultivating self-control is essential for spiritual growth, maturity, wisdom, discipline, and living a Godly life.

Philippians 4:11-13 *Not that I speak in regard to need, for I have learned in whatever state I am, to be content: 12 I know how to be abased, and I know how to abound. Everywhere and in all things I have learned both to be full and to be hungry, both to abound and to suffer need. 13 I can do all things through Christ who strengthens me.*

Hebrews 13:5-6 *5 Let your conduct be without covetousness; be content with such things as you have. For He Himself has said, "I will never leave you nor forsake you." 6 So we may boldly say: "The Lord is my helper; I will not fear. What can man do to me?"*

5. What does it mean to be content? Being content means that when life doesn't turn out like you thought it would you accept it as coming from God for your benefit. It means that you do not get anxious or angry. It means you live a peaceful life free from overreacting to setbacks.

Being content does not mean you should become passive and disengage living life. The Apostle Paul was content but he still had goals, plans, and ambitions.

> Romans 15:22-24 For this reason I also have been much hindered from coming to you. 23 But now no longer having a place in these parts, and having a great desire these many years to come to you, 24 whenever I journey to Spain, I shall come to you. For I hope to see you on my journey, and to be helped on my way there by you, if first I may enjoy your company for a while. 25 But now I am going to Jerusalem to minister to the saints.

6. Believers are to exercise self-control in every area of life. Paul says in I Corinthians 9:25 And everyone who competes for the prize is temperate (self-control) in all things. Now they do it to obtain a perishable crown, but we for an imperishable crown.

PART III "Biblical Principles To Practice For Spiritual Growth" include things for you to practice in order to develop self-control. I know, it's not going to be easy, but it is necessary to grow spiritually. Pick an issue from the list shown below and follow the four steps suggested below.

Trust God No Matter What
Self-Control
How To Deal With Frustration
Do Not Be Anxious.
Do Not Get Angry
Do Not Argue
The Cause and Cure of Depression
How Love Behaves
How to Treat People

7. Four steps to follow to gain self-control. You can use the steps for any issue with witch you are struggling but to illustrate let's use dealing with anger.

A. **Accept responsibility:**
Before you can move toward to a better way of living you must accept responsibility for the choices that you have made. From those choices you developed patterns of thinking, feeling, and behaving that are causing the issue with which you are now struggling.

☐ I struggle with getting angry.

B: **Make the decision to stop:**

Change starts with a decision. You must decide that you want too reverse and overcome the unhealthy patterns you have developed. This sounds simple, or even easy, but it's actually the hardest part! Every person that has changed their behavior first accepted responsibility for what they were doing and decided to change.

☐ I decide to stop getting angry.

C. **Ask God to help you:**

As a Christian, you are not expected to fight the battle by yourself. God wants you call on Him for help. Here are two passages to depend on for God's help.

Hebrews 4:16 *Let us therefore come boldly to the throne of grace, that we may obtain mercy and find grace to help in time of need.*

Proverbs 3:5-7 *Trust in the Lord with all your heart, And lean not on your own understanding; 6 In all your ways acknowledge Him, And He shall direct your paths. 7 Do not be wise in your own eyes; Fear the Lord and depart from evil.*

☐ I ask God to help me to stop getting angry.

D. **Do this every time you get angry:**

As soon as you realize you're angry, stop, ask God to forgive you. Quote this verse **Ephesians 4:31-32** *Let all bitterness, wrath, anger, clamor, and evil speaking be put away from you, with all malice. 32 And be kind to one another, tenderhearted, forgiving one another, even as God in Christ forgave you.*

☐ I will ask for God's forgiveness and stop being angry.

If every time to get angry, and stop, you will eventually be *transformed* according to Romans 12:2 (see pages 53-54). When you are transformed by the work of the Holy Spirit you will no longer want to get angry! It will take time so don't give up.

Repeat these steps for any issue with which you are struggling and you will be transformed and content.

5. How To Deal With Frustration

Frustration can be defined as an *anticipated goal or desire that is left unsatisfied*. It is a feeling of disappointment or exasperation. Of course, everyone has experienced *frustration* during their life.

Simply put, frustration comes from **expectations not met**. We expect people to perform and events to occur. Admittedly, sometimes our expectations are unrealistic or we place too much importance on our expectations.

Expectations not met may cause a series of reactions to occur if each stage is not redirected:

Frustration → Anger → Bitterness → Depression

If your depression is not dealt with it could lead to one or more irrational acts:

☐ Revenge   ☐ Withdrawal   ☐ Irritability

☐ Weeping   ☐ Critical attitude   ☐ Aggression

What is the solution? **Turn the page →**

ADJUST!

As soon as you recognize that you are frustrated (and it may not be immediately obvious to you) say **ADJUST!** to yourself. This will stop the chain of bad feelings from unfolding as mentioned on the previous page. Now think about doing one of the following to end the feeling of frustration:

1. **I choose not to be frustrated.**

   ☐ Everything is a choice.

2. **I will choose another way of looking at what just happened** (I will change my perception).

   ☐ It's not what happened that frustrates me, it's what I think about what happened.

   ☐ How can I look at this so it's not a problem?

   ☐ I will look for a positive/different interpretation of what just happened.

3. **I choose to acknowledge what IS without making a value judgment.**

   ☐ I choose not to jump to conclusions.

   ☐ I choose to be objective and operate on facts.

4. **I choose not to take it personally.**

   ☐ God doesn't do anything to me, He does it for me.

   ☐ Romans 8:28-29   What does God want me to learn?

Now, to help you remember to **ADJUST** make a 3x5 card with **ADJUST** in big letters on one side and put the four ways to **ADJUST** on the other side.

See next page →

ADJUST! 3 X 5 Card

Fill out several 3x5 cards (as illustrated below) to have with you. For example put one in your pocket/ purse, car, desk, etc. Plan to always have one available to remind you what to do. Practice ADJUSTING until you ADJUST automatically. This will take some time so don't give up, plan on ADJUSTING until you no longer get frustrated with people or events.

ADJUST!

1. **I choose Not to Get Frustrated**

   Everything is a choice.

2. **I will change My Perception (Reframe)**

   It's not what happens, it's what I think about what happens.
   How can I look at this so it's not a problem?
   Look for a positive/different interpretation of the event.

3. **I Acknowledge What is Without Making a Value Judgment**

   I will be objective and operate on facts.

4. **I Do Not Take it Personally**

   God doesn't do anything to me, He does it for me.
   Romans 8:28-29 What does God want me to learn?

Maturity

Maturity is directly related to how long it takes you to
respond Biblically (Adjust) to a negative event.

Disturbing Event   Biblical Response

↓   How Long Does It Take You To Adjust   ↓

?

WELL ADJUSTED PEOPLE

1. Not selfish; healthy people can get "outside" of themselves.

    Emotionally healthy people give themselves to something bigger then themselves.

2. Have the ability to have intimacy, love, and compassion.

3. Sufficiently objective about self to know both strengths and weaknesses,

    and has a planned program for overcoming the weaknesses.

4. Willing to adjust; deals with frustration, and irritations without becoming bitter or hostile.

5. Realistic perception; able to see things as they are, not as you wish them to be.

6. Sense of humor; can laugh at self.

7. Unifying philosophy of life; guided by Biblical principles not emotion.

8. Has meaning and direction.

9. Accountable for thoughts, feelings, and actions; takes ownership.

10. Willing to accept what life deals without severe emotional reaction.

If you were to apply this outline you would eventually gain complete control
over that which disturbs you. Consciously and willfully think about
ADJUSTING quickly every time you are frustrated.

The A B C's of Life

What disturbs you is not *what* happens but what the you *think* about what happens. It's not the event, it's what the you think about the event.

A. "People are disturbed, not by things or events, but by the views (perceptions) which they take of them."

Epictetus, 1st Century, A.D.

B. Since then it is my view (perception) that causes me to be disturbed ...

C. What should my view (perception) be so that I'm not disturbed?

A Biblical Perspective:

1. God does not do anything to you, He does it for you.
   Romans 8:28-29

2. How can I look at this so it's not a problem?
   James 1

3. Instead of thinking too much about the wrong thing, focus your thinking on how to solve the problem.
   Philippines 4

4. Answer the question, "what is God's view toward what is upsetting me"?
   Proverbs 3:5-6

Do this:

When you get frustrated, and it lingers for some time, it is because you are rehearsing the painful event over and over. You are focused on the problem. Instead, focus on solving the problem by asking yourself this question, **"How can I look at this so it's not a problem?"** If you focus on solving the problem you will not be thinking about the problem. Write down several ways to solve the problem.

Ephesians 4:32

And be kind to one another, tenderhearted,
forgiving one another, even as God
in Christ forgave you.

6. Do Not Be Anxious
Philippians 4:6-7

Be anxious for nothing, but in everything by prayer and supplication, with thanksgiving, let your requests be made known to God; 7 and the peace of God, which surpasses all understanding, will guard your hearts and minds through Christ Jesus.

It is a **command**, not a suggestion, to *be anxious for nothing*.

When you are feeling anxious about anything, it is because you are not trusting the Lord for the outcome of your concern; the word *anxious* means to be *troubled*.

Here is a breakdown of Philippians 4:6-7.

Do not be anxious about anything,	We are not permitted to worry about anything.
but in every situation,	No exceptions, ever.
by prayer and petition,	Prayer means "to ask"; state your exact concern.
with thanksgiving,	Now, thank God for what He is going to do. Be willing to accept the results as God's will.
present your requests to God.	Be clear, present the requests to God.
the peace of God,	You will have *calm assurance* that God is in control.
which transcends all understanding,	You will no longer be *troubled* or *anxious*.
will guard your hearts and your minds	Your thoughts and feelings will be guarded.

Guard is the greek word *garrison*. Philippi was a military town and they were there to guard (garrison) the area. If you *choose* not to be anxious and you are willing to accept what God will do about your *worry* then He will *guard* your heart. Guard your heart from what? Worry.

The word *heart* here includes mind and emotions. You will have such peace that you will not be able to understand it.

Think Biblically: Philippians 3:5 Be anxious for nothing!

Anxiety Worksheet

1. What is my **anxiety**? Write it below, be specific?

    _____

2. What is the worst that could happen if my **anxiety** is realized?

    _____

3. What is the probability of me coping if the worst happened?

    ☐ Possible   ☐ Impossible

    Why? _____

4. What are three Bible verses that tell me what to do with my **anxiety**?

    ☐ _____

    ☐ _____

    ☐ _____

5. Is my **anxiety** exaggerated?

    ☐ Yes   ☐ No

6. Have I underestimated God's ability to answer my prayer and give me peace?

    ☐ Yes   ☐ No

7. An effective way to deal with my **anxiety** is to:

    ☐ Be fearful and worry.

    ☐ Be anxious for nothing! (Philippians 3:5)

    ☐ Trust God and thank Him for whatever He does.

7. Do Not Get Angry

Ephesians 4:26

Be ye angry and sin not, let not the sun go down on your wrath.

Righteous indignation is a form of anger that is not considered sin. It is an emotional reaction over a sense of injustice like the mistreatment of another person. Jesus, for example, drove the money lenders out of the temple; Matthew 21: 12-13.

All other anger is sin. Consider the following passages:

Proverbs 15:1 *A gentle answer turns away wrath, but a harsh word stirs up anger.*

Proverbs 15:18 *A hot-tempered person stirs up conflict, but the one who is patient calms a quarrel.*

Proverbs 19:19 *A man of great wrath will suffer punishment; For if you rescue him, you will have to do it again.*

Ecclesiastes 7:9 Do not be quickly provoked in your spirit, for anger resides in the lap of fools.

I Corinthians 13:5 *Love is not provoked.*

Ecclesiastes 7:9 *Do not hasten in your spirit to be angry, For anger rests in the bosom of fools.*

Believers are not allowed to get angry but if you do, God says deal with it quickly; before the sun goes down. Anger harms relationships and divides.

The Fence

There once was a young boy with a very bad temper. The boy's father wanted to teach him a lesson so he gave him a bag of nails and told him that every time he lost his temper he must hammer a nail into their wooden fence.

On the first day of this lesson the little boy had driven 37 nails into the fence. He was really mad! Over the course of the next few weeks the little boy began to control his temper so the number of nails that were hammered into the fence dramatically decreased.

Pleased, his father suggested that he now pull out one nail for each day that he could hold his temper.

Several weeks went by and the day finally came when the young boy was able to tell his father that all the nails were gone. Very gently the father took his son by the hand and led him to the fence. "You have done very well my son," he smiled, "But look at the holes in the fence. The fence will never be the same." The little boy listened carefully as his father continued to speak.

"When you say things in anger they leave permanent scars just like these. And no matter how many times you say you're sorry the wounds will still be there."

Think Biblically

Ephesians 4:26 *Be ye angry and sin not, let not the sun go down on your wrath.*

8. Do Not Argue

Proverbs 17:14

1. **Arguing damages relationships.**

A major theme of failing relationships is arguing. What the argument centers on varies from minor to major. It doesn't matter what the disagreement is over, what matters is that the issue becomes a problem. Instead of discussing a matter objectively two people engage in making, proving, or defending their point. The goal becomes winning your point instead of coming to an agreement and the relationship is damaged. Don't think that the damage is for a moment, but in fact the damage can last for years. Routine arguing leaves a residue of resentment that builds up over time and will eventually reduce the feelings you have for the other person or destroy the relationship completely.

2. Control your emotions.

Proverbs 15:18 A hot-tempered man stirs up dissension, but a patient man calms a quarrel.

Proverbs 17:14 Starting a quarrel is like breaching a dam; so drop the matter before a dispute breaks out.

Proverbs 17:19 *He who loves a quarrel loves sin; he who builds a high gate invites destruction.*

Proverbs 16:32 *Better to be patient than powerful; better to have self-control than to conquer a city.*

Ephesians 4:29 *Let no corrupt communication proceed out of your mouth, but that which is good to the use of edifying, that it may minister grace unto the hearers.*

Ephesians 4:2 *Be ye angry and sin not, let not the sun go down on your wrath.*

3. Love doesn't argue. I Corinthians 13: 4-8

Love is **patient**: Love never takes the opportunity to avenge itself.
Love is **not provoked**: Love does not get irritated.
Love **does not seek its own**: Love does not trade being right for another person's feelings.
Love is **kind**: Love never offends, insults or says anything unkind.

4. Keep the peace:

God places a high value on keeping the peace. When you participate in an argument you are contributing to disturbing the peace. It is Christ-like not to argue about anything.

Romans 12:18 *If it is possible, as far as it depends on you, live at peace with everyone.*

II Thessalonians 3:16 *Now may the Lord of peace himself give you peace at all times in every way. The Lord be with you all.*

Matthew 5:9 *Blessed are the peacemakers, for they shall be called sons of God.*

John 14:27 *Peace I leave with you; my peace I give to you. Not as the world gives do I give to you. Let not your hearts be troubled, neither let them be afraid.*

Hebrews 12:14 *Strive for peace with everyone, and for the holiness without which no one will see the Lord.*

I Corinthians 14:33 *For God is not a God of confusion but of peace. As in all the churches of the saints,*

I Peter 3:9-11 *Do not repay evil for evil or reviling for reviling, but on the contrary, bless, for to this you were called, that you may obtain a blessing. For "Whoever desires to love life and see good days, let him keep his tongue from evil and his lips from speaking deceit; let him turn away from evil and do good; let him seek peace and pursue it.*

The message is clear, do not argue, keep the peace.

Think Biblically:

Do not argue, remember Proverbs 17:14
Starting a quarrel is like breaching a dam;
so drop the matter before a dispute breaks out.

9. Two Kinds of Guilt

1. True guilt.

You have committed sin. I John 1:8-10

> If we claim to be without sin, we deceive ourselves and the truth is not in us. If we confess our sins, he is faithful and just and will forgive us our sins and purify us from all unrighteousness. If we claim we have not sinned, we make him out to be a liar and his word is not in us.

2. False guilt.

You have confessed your sin to the Lord but you still feel guilty. When guilty feelings arise over sins already confessed, reject such feelings as <u>false guilt</u>.

God has forgiven you. Read and meditate on Psalm 103:8-12.

> *The LORD is compassionate and gracious, slow to anger, abounding in love. He will not always accuse, nor will he harbor his anger forever; he does not treat us as our sins deserve or repay us according to our iniquities. For as high as the heavens are above the earth, so great is his love for those who fear him;* **as far as the east is from the west, so far has he removed our transgressions from us**.

3. When guilt feelings linger.

When guilt feelings linger after confessing the sin consider these two options:

A. You may need to go to the person that you sinned against and ask forgiveness and make restitution. For example, if you stole something you should return it to the owner.

B. If guilt feelings linger and there is no one to go to then it is pride. Pride keeps the focus on "you" and what "you" have done. The focus should be on "Him" and what "He" has done. He paid the price for your sin and promised to forgive you if you confess you sin. Since He has forgiven you and has separated your sin as far as the East is from the West, what right do you have to hold on to that which has been forgiven?

Think Biblically: God does not hold onto it and neither should you!

Proverbs 15:1

A gentle answer turns away wrath,
but a harsh word stirs up anger.

10. The Cause and Cure of Depression

Proverbs 12:25

Anxiety in the heart of man causes depression,
But a good word makes it glad.

There are only two reasons that a person gets depressed.

1. A chemical imbalance in your brain.

    There is no scientific evidence that a chemical imbalance in the brain exists that causes depression. It's only a theory. See my book *Man's Wisdom or God's Wisdom* for a treatment of the chemical imbalance theory; available online at Amazon and Barnes and Noble.

    Note: Postpartum depression often suffered by a mother after childbirth, is typically due to hormonal changes, psychological adjustment to motherhood, and fatigue.

2. You are thinking too much about the wrong thing.

    Some Christians respond to their unpleasant circumstances by becoming depressed. Depression is a feeling of sadness and dejection that alters a person's emotional and mental state and interferes with their daily life functions in varying degrees. Symptoms range from mild to severe and can be short-term or last for an extended period.

    Before I go further please understand that some down feelings are not only appropriate but normal. For example, if you were to lose a loved one to death it would be expected to feel deeply sad emotions and have normal activities like eating, sleeping, and working interrupted. After some time has elapsed these functions return to normal and we continue our journey through this life.

    For the most part, however, those who report they are "depressed" are focused on one or more problems. Life has overwhelmed them, a tragic event has happen, or something did not happened as expected, someone did something to them, or they did something to someone else ... the list is endless.

    It is different however when a Christian *routinely* gets depressed over the painful events in their life. It is different when the Christian retreats and withdraws from life to pout or fume about their circumstances. It is different when a Christian reacts negatively to events, gets angry, and depressed.

    When depression is a routine response to life's circumstances people are living examples of what Epictetus said 2,000 years ago (as mentioned earlier). Epictetus said that it is not *what* happened to you that is disturbing, it is what you *think about* what happened that is disturbing you.

Depressed people disturb themselves by holding on to their negative perception of the event. If you are depressed you are not trying to solve the problem, you are embedded in the problem by reviewing the negatives and fuming over the wrongness of the event. If you are routinely depressed you are choosing to be miserable.

If you often react this way it is because you fail to see that God is working through your circumstances to conform you into the image of His Son (Romans 8:28-29). Instead of seeing God in the situation you are viewing your circumstance as not fair, wrong, or even punishment from God. The unfairness or wrongness is what is being reviewed and rehearsed in your thoughts. All you can see is the pain and suffering you are going through and you want it to stop ... now! You are stuck in, and focused on, the problem. You fail to see or do not accept what God is doing in your life through your circumstances.

Depression and Scripture

The Bible was written over a sixteen-hundred-year period and from the beginning God had something to say about being depressed.

Deuteronomy 31:8 It is the LORD who goes before you. He will be with you; he will not leave you or forsake you. Do not fear or be dismayed.

The Hebrew word translated leave has the idea of leave alone. The word that immediately follows is forsake which means to leave destitute or fail. The Hebrew word translated dismayed means to break down, either (literally) by violence, or (figuratively) by confusion and fear; to beat down, caused to be discourage.

So Moses, the writer of Deuteronomy, has given us three reasons to not be discouraged or depressed. First, God goes before you which means He holds the future and He is leading you. Second, He is with you which means He is beside you. Thirdly, He will never fail you or leave you destitute.

With promises like this, there is no reason to ever be discouraged or depressed. God is there for you and always will be. God continued to encourage us throughout the Bible to wait on Him, to hope in Him, and to humble ourselves before Him as noted in the following verses:

Psalms 40:1-3 I waited patiently for the LORD; he inclined to me and heard my cry. He drew me up from the pit of destruction, out of the miry bog, and set my feet upon a rock, making my steps secure. He put a new song in my mouth, a song of praise to our God. Many will see and fear, and put their trust in the LORD.

1 Peter 5:6-7 Humble yourselves therefore under the mighty hand of God, that he may exalt you in due time: Casting all your care upon him; for he careth for you.

Think Biblically: Trust God that He is working in all of your circumstances.

11. How Loves Behave

I Corinthians 13:4-8

Love suffers long and is kind; love does not envy; love does not parade itself, is not puffed up; 5 does not behave rudely, does not seek its own, is not provoked, thinks no evil; 6 does not rejoice in iniquity, but rejoices in the truth; 7 bears all things, believes all things, hopes all things, endures all things.

1. Love is PATIENT - **Love never takes the opportunity to avenge itself.**

2. Love is KIND - **Love never offends, insults or says anything unkind.**

3. Love is NOT JEALOUS - Love does not desire what another person has in an evil way.

4. Love DOES NOT BRAG - Love does not draw attention to itself.

5. Love is NOT PUFFED UP - Love does not have a superior attitude.

6. Love is NOT RUDE - **Love has good manners and makes you feel comfortable.**

7. Love SEEKS NOT ITS OWN - **Love does not trade being right for another person's feelings.**

8. Love is NOT PROVOKED - **Love does not get irritated.**

9. Love THINKS NO EVIL - Love does not keep an account of evil deeds, it forgives.

10. Love DOES NOT REJOICE OVER ANOTHER'S FAULT - Love rejoices in the truth.

11. Love COVERS SIN - **Love is able to overlook any sin**.

12. Love ALWAYS BELIEVES THE BEST - Love looks at facts, not rumors.

13. Love ALWAYS LOOKS ON THE BRIGHT SIDE - Love is never pessimistic.

14. Love SUSTAINS YOU THROUGH SUFFERING - Love remains steadfast in the face of unpleasant circumstances.

15. Love WILL NEVER RUN IN DEFEAT - Love never gives up.

A Summary of I Corinthians 13:4-8 by Dr. Tom Constable

Love does not deal with other people in a way that injures their dignity. It does not insist on having its own way, nor does it put it's own interest before the needs of others. Love is not irritable or touchy, and it **absorbs** offenses, insults, and inconveniences for the sake of others' welfare. It does not keep a record of offenses received to pay them back.

Think Biblically: Love others.

12. How To Treat People

How you treat others is a reflection of your spiritual maturity. Spiritual growth is the result of applying Biblical truth to your life. It requires, as James directs us in 1:22, to be *"doers of the Word and not hears only."*

It is necessary to know the truth of Scripture but knowing is not enough, one must *do* what the Scripture requires before growth occurs.

> Many years ago I was counseling a couple that were having difficulties in their relationship. The current issue was that the wife was angry at her husband and would not forgive him. You would have thought he was guilty of something so horrific that God Himself would have trouble forgiving him. She was that angry! Before I go further, I have been given permission to share this story.
>
> What did he do that was so unforgiving? He cleaned the house when she wasn't there! Really! Now according to the husband, the house was in need of a serious cleaning. It had been neglected, like their two young daughters, for many months. She would stay out to the early morning hours with her friends from work. To make matters worse, the husband asked his parents to help. That was the core of her problem because she was embarrassed.
>
> Nothing I said made a difference. I then asked, "Do you want God to treat you like you treat other people (implying her husband)? She quickly said No!" I shared with her the way God treats all of us and we are to do the same with other people. Here is what I said:

A. He Loves You Unconditionally

The Bible is clear about God's love. He loves you unconditionally and nothing can separate you from His love. It is because of God's love for you that brought you to salvation.

John 3:16 *For God so loved the world that He gave His One and only Son, that whoever believes in Him shall not perish but have eternal life.*

Romans 8:38-39 *For I am convinced that neither death nor life, neither angels nor demons, neither the present nor the future, nor any powers, neither height nor depth, nor anything else in all creation, will be able to separate us from the love of God that is in Christ Jesus our Lord.*

Because God has demonstrated His love toward us we are to therefore show the same kind of love to other people. God loves us without conditions. We do not have *to do* this or that, or *not do* this or that, in order for God to love us. He loves us regardless of what we do, or not do. Every time we sin He is ready to forgive and restore. Not nearly every time, but every time!

B. He Forgives You Freely

Remember, God loved you so much that He forgave you of all your sin when you became a believer. Therefore ...

Ephesians 4:32 *Be kind and compassionate to one another, forgiving each other, just as in Christ, God forgave you.*

> What can anyone do to you that is greater than what you and I did to Christ? Because of your sin and my sin He went to the cross. What right do you have, or me, to not forgive someone when Jesus has forgiven us of much greater sin? There are no conditions or limits to forgiveness.

> Matthew 18:21-22 Then Peter came up and said to Him, "Lord, how often will my brother sin against me, and I forgive him? As many as seven times?" Jesus said to him, "I do not say to you seven times, but seventy times seven.

> Jesus is saying that forgiveness has no conditions or limits. Continue to forgive, again, and again, and again, keep on forgiving. That's the way God treats you.

C. He Shows You Unlimited Grace

God shows us Grace regardless of what we have done. There is an amazing truth in the story of our Lord's crucifixion and resurrection.

> Mark's record of the account (14:66 -16:20) tells how Peter denied the Lord three times the night before He was crucified. When the three women arrived at the tomb three days later to anoint Jesus with spices they discovered that He was gone. An angel told them that He is risen! Then, the angel told them to go tell the disciples ... and Peter!
>   What a demonstration of God's Grace! Peter had denied the Lord three times before He was crucified and God The Father told the angel to tell Mary to be sure to tell **Peter**!

God showed Grace to Peter after His darkest moment. God shows that same Grace to you. Show the same Grace to others.

Think Biblically: Remember Ephesians 4:32, Show Grace to others every chance you get.

Chapter 7

How To Know If You Are Growing Spiritually

Growing spiritually means you are becoming like Christ, thinking as He thinks, behaving as He did. The evidence of spiritual growth is in the fruit of the Spirit being demonstrated in the way you live your life. This passage gives you a check list from which you can compare your behavior.

> Galatians 5:22-23 But the fruit of the Spirit is love, joy, peace, longsuffering, kindness, goodness, faithfulness, gentleness, self-control. Against such there is no law.

1. **Love** - The Greek word for love in this passage is *agape* which is self-sacrificing affection for others.

   ☐ Love people according to I Corinthians 13:5-8 (pages 75-76).

2. **Joy** - Means *calm delight* which is deep-seated gladness regardless of your circumstances. Calm delight is the result of **knowing** that God is working in your circumstances.

   James 1:2 *My brethren, count it all **joy** [have calm delight] when you fall into various trials.*

   ☐ I will have "calm delight" when I am in a trial because I believe God is at work for my benefit.

3. **Peace** - This is an inward tranquility and serenity that comes from knowing you are trusting God for what He is doing in your life. It's inner quietness regardless of your circumstances.

   Col 3:15 *Let the peace of God rule in your heart.*

   ☐ I have "peace" in my heart knowing God is at work in my circumstances.

4. **Longsuffering** - Means *patience* even under provocation or in the face of trails.

   James 1:4 *but let endurance (patience) have its complete work, that you may be complete and mature, lacking nothing.*

   ☐ I will be patient with others and in trials because God is patient with me.

5. **Kindness** - Kindness in action is sweetness of disposition, gentleness in dealing with others, graciousness.

> **Ephesians 2:7** *that in the ages to come He might show the exceeding riches of His grace in His kindness toward us in Christ Jesus.*

> ☐ I will be kind to others because God is kind to me.

6. **Goodness** - Constructive action reaching out to others, goodness of words and deeds.

> **Galatians 6:10** *As we have therefore opportunity, let us do good unto all men, especially unto them who are of the household of faith.*

> ☐ I will be good to others because God is good to me.

7. **Faithfulness** - Means dependability, loyalty, stability, worthy of trust.

> **Proverbs 28:20** *A faithful man will abound with blessings, But he who makes haste to be rich will not go unpunished.*

> ☐ I will be faithful to God because God is faithful to me.

8. **Meekness** - Strength under control. A disposition that is even-tempered, gentle, tranquil, balanced in spirit, unpretentious, and has passions under control.

> **Titus 3:2** *To speak evil of no one, to avoid quarreling, to be gentle, and to show perfect courtesy toward all people.*

> ☐ I will be gentle to others because God is gentle to me.

9. **Self-control** - is mastery of one's thoughts, feelings, behavior, desires, speech, and impulses (see pages 55-58).

> **Proverbs 16:32** *Better a patient person than a warrior, one with **self-control** than one who takes a city.*

> ☐ I will diligently work at controlling my thoughts, feelings, behavior, speech, desires, and impulses.

How might your temperament affect your spiritual growth? Ultimately it's a person's heart, not temperament, that determines spiritual desire and growth.

Psalm 37:4 Delight yourself also in the Lord, And He shall give you the desires of your heart.

Your temperament, however, can have a significant impact on how you pursue spiritual growth. Every temperament blend must challenge and overcome some of their natural tendencies to grow spiritually.

Challenges

Lack of motivation: You tend to avoid challenges or strong emotional engagement. This can lead to complacency and a lack of drive in pursuing spiritual growth, as you might not feel urgency or excitement about making changes.

Avoidance of conflict: You might be content to avoid difficult conversations or emotional confrontations, which will prevent you from facing deeper spiritual questions or working through personal issues that would lead to growth.

Passivity: You tend to be more passive in your approach to life, waiting for things to come to you rather than actively pursuing spiritual practices or seeking out opportunities for deeper understanding. Spiritual growth requires initiative, discipline, and persistence.

Overemphasis on comfort: You often focus on stability and peace and avoid pushing yourself out of your comfort zone which will limit your spiritual development. Growth requires stepping into uncomfortable or unfamiliar territory.

Difficulty with passion or zeal: You are steady and reliable so you may not experience the same intensity or fervor for spiritual practices that others might. Without that fire, spiritual disciplines like prayer, study, or service to others might feel less engaging.

Limited self-reflection: You are more laid-back so you tend to avoid confronting internal struggles. Spiritual growth requires self-reflection and introspection which you might not naturally prioritize.

Spiritual growth involves altering your natural tendencies with disciplines that result in control of what you think, feel, say, and do.

Potential

Once you establish a level of spiritual growth your nature to have a routine will hold you steady. Seek opportunities to serve others and do it as unto the Lord.

Ecclesiastes 9:10 Whatever your hand finds to do, do it with all your might.

Growing spiritually requires time, actually a *life* time. The Apostle Peter encouraged Christians to grow knowing it takes time.

2 Peter 3:18 *grow in the grace and knowledge of our Lord and Savior Jesus Christ.*

The word "grow" in this passage is used to depict the growth of a plant or infant both of which takes time to grow. So don't be hard on yourself if you are not making the progress you expected. Do not give up. Keep working on practicing the fruit of the Spirit, loving others, and doing the other things in this workbook. Remember, it takes time to be transformed.

Dr. Henry Brandt

A mature man is one who is sufficiently objective about himself
to know both his strengths and his weaknesses and to create
a planned program for overcoming his weaknesses.

Think Biblically

Recommend Books

Cocoris, John T. *Why We Do What We Do, New Insights Into The Temperament Model of Behavior.* McKinney, Texas: Temperament Dynamics LLC, 2020.

_____. *Born with a Creative Temperament.* McKinney, TX: Temperament Dynamics LLC, 2014.

_____. *Seven Steps to a Better You.* McKinney, TX: Temperament Dynamics LLC, 2014.

_____. *A Parent's Guide to Helping Your Child Develop Their Natural Temperament Tendencies.* McKinney, TX: Temperament Dynamics LLC, 2016.

_____. *Trust God No Matter What.* McKinney, TX: Temperament Dynmics LLC, 2025.

_____. *Man's Wisdom or God's Wisdom, The Cause And Cure Of Mental, Emotional, And Behavior Issues.* McKinney, TX: Temperament Dynamics LLC, 2025.

_____. *Three Reasons Christians Go To Counseling.* McKinney, TX: Temperament Dynmics LLC, 2015.

_____. *Why Girls Chase Guys After A Breakup.* McKinney, TX: Temp. Dynamics, LLC, 2020.

Cocoris, G. Michael. *Spiritual Basics: Basic Biblical Truths for Living a Spiritual Life.* Santa Monica, CA: J and M Brothers Publications, 2025.

_____. *The Spiritual Life: Clarifying the Confusion.* Santa Monica, CA: J and M Brothers Publications, 2011, 2018.

_____. *Counseling Theories, A Simple Explanation And Biblical Evaluation.* Santa Monica, CA: J and M Brothers Publications, 2024.

Temperament Blend Workbooks

Cocoris, John T. *Choleric-Sanguine Workbook: The Executive Pattern, How To Develop Your Natural Tendencies And Deal With Your Strengths And Weaknesses Biblically.* McKinney, Texas: Temperament Dynamics, LLC, 2025.

_____ *Choleric-Phlegmatic Workbook: The Director Pattern, How To Develop Your Natural Tendencies And Deal With Your Strengths And Weaknesses Biblically.* McKinney, Texas: Temperament Dynamics, LLC, 2025.

_____ *Choleric-Melancholy Workbook: The Strategist Pattern, How To Develop Your Natural Tendencies And Deal With Your Strengths And Weaknesses Biblically.* McKinney, Texas: Temperament Dynamics, LLC, 2025.

_____ *Sanguine-Choleric Workbook The Negotiator Pattern, How To Develop Your Natural Tendencies And Deal With Your Strengths And Weaknesses Biblically.* McKinney, Texas: Temperament Dynamics, LLC, 2025.

_____ *Sanguine-Phlegmatic Workbook: The Relater Pattern, How To Develop Your Natural Tendencies And Deal With Your Strengths And Weaknesses Biblically.* McKinney, Texas: Temperament Dynamics, LLC, 2025.

_____ *Sanguine-Melancholy Workbook: The Performer Pattern, How To Develop Your Natural Tendencies And Deal With Your Strengths And Weaknesses Biblically.* McKinney, Texas: Temperament Dynamics, LLC, 2025.

_____. *Phlegmatic-Choleric Workbook: The Inspector Pattern, How To Develop Your Natural Tendencies And Deal With Your Strengths And Weaknesses Biblically.* McKinney, Texas: Temperament Dynamics, LLC, 2025.

_____. *Phlegmatic-Sanguine Workbook: The Harmonizer Pattern, How To Develop Your Natural Tendencies And Deal With Your Strengths And Weaknesses Biblically.* McKinney, Texas: Temperament Dynamics, LLC, 2025.

_____. *Phlegmatic-Melancholy Workbook: Helper Pattern, How To Develop Your Natural Tendencies And Deal With Your Strengths And Weaknesses Biblically.* McKinney, Texas: Temperament Dynamics, LLC, 2025.

_____. *Melancholy-Choleric Workbook: The Instructor Pattern, How To Develop Your Natural Tendencies And Deal With Your Strengths And Weaknesses Biblically.* McKinney, Texas: Temperament Dynamics, LLC, 2025.

_____. *Melancholy-Sanguine Workbook: The Diplomat Pattern, How To Develop Your Natural Tendencies And Deal With Your Strengths And Weaknesses Biblically.* McKinney, Texas: Temperament Dynamics, LLC, 2025.

_____. *Melancholy-Phlegmatic Workbook: The Analyst Pattern, How To Develop Your Natural Tendencies And Deal With Your Strengths And Weaknesses Biblically.* McKinney, Texas: Temperament Dynamics, LLC, 2025.

About The Author

John T. Cocoris has devoted his life since the 1970s to develop the temperament model of behavior. John has a B.A. from Tennessee Temple University, a Masters of Theology (Th. M.) from Dallas Theological Seminary, a Masters in Counseling (M.A.) from Amberton University, and a Doctorate in Psychology (Psy.D.) from California Coast University. John was a licensed therapist in the state of Texas from 1995-2020.

John established Profile Dynamics in the early 1980s to develop and promote the temperament model of behavior for use in business and counseling. He has been a management consultant since 1984 and has worked with a variety of companies giving seminars for training managers and sales people.

John has conducted seminars in churches to help church counselors help others. John has also trained other therapists in the use of the temperament model in counseling. John has been interviewed on the radio and has been featured numerous times on COPE, a national cable TV talk show.

John and Phillip Moss formed Temperament Dynamics, LLC in 2017 to further develop, expand, and promote the temperament model of behavior.

John has written many books and manuals about the temperament model including: *Why We Do What We Do, New Insights Into The Temperament Model of Behavior; Born With A Creative Temperament, The Sanguine-Melancholy; 7 Steps To A Better You, How To Develop Your Natural Tendencies; A Parent's Manual To Helping Your Child Develop Their Natural Temperament Tendencies; A Therapist's Guide to The Temperament Model of Behavior; A Leader's Guide To Using The Temperament Model of Behavior; How To Sell Using The Temperament Model of Behavior; The* DISCII, DISC3, *DISC Strengths, and Four Temperaments Assessments, and The Temperament Profile Assessment User's Guide.*

www.ingramcontent.com/pod-product-compliance
Lightning Source LLC
Chambersburg PA
CBHW080424030426

42335CB00020B/2575